GOD, PHILOSOPHY
AND
ACADEMIC CULTURE

AAR

American Academy of Religion
Reflection and Theory in the Study of Religion

Editor
David E. Klemm

Number 11
GOD, PHILOSOPHY AND ACADEMIC CULTURE
A Discussion between Scholars in the AAR and the APA

edited by
William J. Wainwright

GOD, PHILOSOPHY
AND
ACADEMIC CULTURE

A Discussion between Scholars in the
AAR and the APA

edited by
William J. Wainwright

Scholars Press
Atlanta, Georgia

GOD, PHILOSOPHY
AND
ACADEMIC CULTURE
A Discussion between Scholars in the
AAR and the APA

edited by
William J. Wainwright

© 1996
The American Academy of Religion

BL
51
.G684
1996

Library of Congress Cataloging in Publication Data

God, Philosophy, and academic culture : a discussion between scholars
in the AAR and the APA / edited by William J. Wainwright.
  p. cm. — (AAR reflection and theory in the study of religion
; no. 11)
    ISBN 0-7885-0301-4 (cloth : alk. paper). — ISBN 0-7885-0302-2
(pbk. : alk. paper)
    1. Religion—Philosophy—Congresses. 2. Religion—Philosophy—
Study and teaching—United States—History—20th century—
Congresses. 3. American Academy of Religion—Congresses.
4. American Philosophical Association—Congresses. I. Wainwright,
William J. II. Series.
BL51.G684   1996
210—dc20   96-28727
                                                       CIP

Printed in the United States of America
on acid-free paper

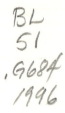

Table of Contents

Contributors

Robert M. Adams is chair of the Department of Philosophy at Yale University. A number of his essays on the history of philosophy, moral philosophy, metaphysics, and the philosophy of religion have been collected in *The Virtue of Faith and Other Essays in Philosophical Theology* (1987). His most recent book is *Leibniz: Determinist, Theist, Idealist* (1994).

Stephen Crites is Professor of Philosophy at Wesleyan University. He is the editor of Kierkegaard's *Crisis in the Life of an Actress and Other Essays on Drama* (1967), and the author of *In the Twilight of Christendom: Hegel vs. Kierkegaard on Faith and History* (1972) and *Religion as Story* (1975). He is currently working on a book entitled *The Aesthetic Formation of Experience*.

C. Stephen Evans is William Spoelhof Scholar and Professor of Philosophy at Calvin College. His publications include *Subjectivity and Religious Belief* (1978), *Kierkegaard's Fragments*: *The Religious Philosophy of Johannes Climacus* (1983), *Soren Kierkegaard's Christian Psychology* (1990), and *Passionate Reason: Making Sense of Kierkegaard's Philosophical Fragments* (1992).

Walter Lowe is Professor of Systematic Theology at Emory University. He has written in the area of hermeneutics with particular attention to Kant, Freud, Ricoeur, and Derrida. He is the author of *Evil and the Unconscious* (1983) and *Theology and Difference: The Wound of Reason* (1993).

Wayne Proudfoot is Professor of Religion at Columbia University. His publications include *God and the Self: Three Types of Philosophy of Religion* (1976) and *Religious Experience* (1985). He has recently co-edited *Faithful Imagining: Essays in Honor of Richard R. Niebuhr* (1995).

Philip L. Quinn is John A. O'Brian Professor of Philosophy at the University of Notre Dame, a former editor of *Faith and Philosophy*, and a recent president of the Central Division of the American Philosophical Association. He is the author of *Divine Commands and Moral Requirements* (1978) and numerous articles in philosophy of religion, philosophy of science, and metaphysics.

William J. Wainwright is Professor of Philosophy at the University of Wisconsin-Milwaukee and current editor of *Faith and Philosophy*. His publications include *Philosophy of Religion: An Annotated Bibliography*. (1978), *Mysticism* (1981), *Philosophy of Religion* (1988), and *Reason and the Heart* (1995).

Merold Westphal is Professor of Philosophy at Fordham University. Recent publications include *Kierkegaard's Critique of Reason and Society* (1987), *Hegel, Freedom and Modernity* (1992), *Suspicion and Faith: The Religious Uses of Modern Atheism* (1993), and *Modernity and its Discontents* (1992) and *Kierkegaard in Post-Modernity* (1995) of which he is co-editor.

Nicholas Wolterstorff is Professor of Philosophical Theology at the Divinity School of Yale University and a past president of the Central Division of the American Philosophical Association. Major publications include *On Universals: An Essay in Ontology* (1970), *Works and Worlds of Art* (1980), *Divine Discourse: Philosophical Reflections on the Claim that God Speaks* (1995), and *John Locke and the Ethics of Belief* (1996).

Introduction

William J. Wainwright

I studied philosophy at Kenyon College and at the University of Michigan. My training in both institutions was primarily analytic. I still regard myself as an analytic philosopher in the broad sense. My first published papers in the philosophy of religion were on the verification controversy. From the late sixties through the mid-eighties, I primarily published in two areas—philosophical theology and the epistemology of mystical experience. My most recent work has been on the epistemic status of the heart's influence on reasoning about what Jonathan Edwards calls "divine things."

The American Philosophical Association has been my principal professional association throughout my career. But in the mid-seventies I was invited to join the Cross-Cultural Philosophy of Religion Group of the American Academy of Religion. When that disbanded, I was asked to serve on the steering committee of the Philosophy of Religion Section. I have now faithfully attended meetings of the AAR for twenty years. My association with it has been stimulating. I have learned much from my colleagues in theology, the history of religions, and related disciplines.

One of the first things I noticed on joining the AAR, however, was how few of my colleagues in the APA belonged to it or attended its meetings. Indeed, some of the best known and most widely respected analytic philosophers of religion were only vaguely aware of its existence. I soon discovered that this ignorance or lack of interest was mutual. Most AAR members who identify themselves as philosophers of religion do not belong to the APA. Many of them are only superficially familiar with the persons and topics that figure so prominently in the philosophy of religion sessions of its annual meetings and in the journals in which APA philosophers publish.

As a member of the Philosophy of Religion Section's steering committee, I have worked to heal this breach. Over the years, Alvin Plantinga, William Rowe, William Alston, Philip Quinn, Eleanore Stump, Robert Adams, and other prominent analytic philosophers of religion have participated in symposia at our annual meetings. These sessions have been well attended and, by all accounts, successful. The chair and other members of the steering committee have supported these efforts. But our success has been limited, and the gap between APA philosophers of religion and their counterparts in the AAR remains. So the question is, why does it exist and what can be done to overcome it?

But something else also soon struck me on joining the AAR. Most APA philosophers of religion are theists or (if they are not) take only theism seriously. It seems fair to say that most AAR philosophers of religion are not theists. Or in any case, that the proportion of philosophers of religion who are theists is much smaller in the AAR than in the APA. I wondered why this was true, and whether the different attitudes towards theism were connected to the different ways in which APA and AAR philosophers of religion typically practice their discipline.

In 1993 William Dean, who was then chair of the steering committee of the Philosophy of Religion Section, asked me to organize a panel addressing these issues. Seeking to strike a balance between analytic and non-analytic philosophers, and between philosophers who were primarily affiliated with the APA and philosophers who were not, I invited Merold Westphal, Nicholas Wolterstorff, Walter Lowe, and Stephen Crites. The panel turned out to be even more successful than we had anticipated. The audience was large, and many who attended expressed a wish to continue the discussion. It was clear that the questions the panelists addressed had struck a nerve. The present volume is a direct outgrowth of that session and of the enthusiasm it generated.

A striking feature of the papers that follow is that the authors largely agree about the causes of the split. There is considerably less agreement as to how the differences in practice, attitude, commitment, and socialization which have caused the split should be evaluated. What is encouraging, however, is each side's recognition that it has things to learn from the other.

One of the conclusions which emerges from these papers is that the differences which were the occasion for this volume are correlated with other differences which are important for understanding them. First, APA philosophers of religion are usually housed in departments of philosophy. AAR philosophers of religion are typically housed in departments of religion. Second, Philip Quinn reminds us that analytic philosophy as currently practiced assumes that one can distinguish true from false propositions in a principled way. As a result, analytic philosophers tend to focus on the truth or falsity of the claims they investigate. Since analytic philosophy dominates most departments of philosophy and the APA, it is hardly surprising that few APA philosophers of religion are relativists. By contrast, what Wolterstorff calls "interpretation universalism" pervades the AAR. According to this view, *everything* is interpretation. "Things exist and are as they are only relative to one or another of our conceptual schemes." Third,

Lowe calls our attention to the fact that whereas APA philosophers of religion tend to focus on God or the religious object, AAR philosophers of religion tend to focus on religion and the human subject. Finally, and unlike most (though not all) APA philosophers of religion, AAR philosophers of religion are especially concerned with the relation between religion and ethics. "Examples," according to Lowe, "would include much reflection which proceeds under the heading of 'liberation' and much which seeks to represent various marginalized voices."

These differences are real and perhaps obvious. What is not so obvious is how we are to account for them. Hopefully, the essays in this volume will provide some help.

Nicholas Wolterstorff suggests that the liberalism that dominates the academy partly explains religion departments' tendency to exclude theistic voices. Classical liberalism insists that private or sectarian visions of the world and the human good must be excluded from the public arena. Public authority should be neutral between competing conceptions of the good. This neutral authority has been identified historically with reason and common experience. But the conviction that religious world-views can't be established by reason or common experience pervades the academy. The result is to restrict the role of religion in public universities (and in the private universities and colleges which emulate them) to the study *of* religion. Its *espousal* is largely excluded.

The dominance of liberalism thus helps explain the academy's hostility to open espousals of theism. But it doesn't explain why departments of religious studies should be more hostile to open espousals of theism than to open espousals of, say, Buddhism. Nor does it explain why departments of philosophy should be less hostile to evangelicals and other traditional theists than departments of religious studies are. (For both are parts of the academy.) Wolterstorff suggests that the modern academy's suspicion of power together with theism's hegemonic position in western culture helps explain the first. Merold Westphal's essay helps explain the second.

Westphal calls our attention to the delicate position of religious studies departments in public and private universities and colleges. Because of the suspicion of religion which pervades our colleges and universities, and the fact that departments of religious studies are recent and therefore fragile growths, there is a tendency to play it safe by excluding voices which are "likely to offend the prevailing ethos in the academy." These most notably include fundamentalists, evangelicals, and other traditional theists. The dynamics in question have not affected philosophy departments to the same extent. (Although as Stephen Evans points out, hostility towards theists and theism is by no means unknown in departments of philosophy.[1]) Philosophy has been part of the academy since its inception, and is not regarded as problematic. Philosophy of religion is a recognized subdiscipline within philosophy like aesthetics or the philosophy of science and thus shares philosophy's non-problematic status. In addition, those who do philosophy of religion typically prove their worth to colleagues in other branches of philosophy by doing important work in other (perhaps less suspect) areas. Alvin Plantinga and William Alston in epistemology, for example, or Nicholas Wolterstorff in aesthetics and the history of philosophy. And finally, as Robert Adams points out, theism is deeply embedded in the philosophical classics which students of philosophy are expected to master and that continue to nourish the western philosophical tradition.

Another reason why theists often feel more at home in departments of philosophy than in departments of religious studies may be this. Traditional theists can embrace continental thought and work within its traditions. Merold Westphal and Stephen Evans are good examples. But an interpretation universalism which has its roots in Nietzsche pervades much recent continental philosophy. And it is at least unclear that traditional theists can adopt interpretation universalism or be relativists. Analytic philosophy, by and large, rejects these trends, retaining a certain confidence in reason's ability to adjudicate claims of truth and falsity. It isn't surprising, therefore, that philosophers of religion who are also traditional theists are more likely to find the analytic approach to philosophy congenial than that of, say, Derrida. In addition, "in its intellectual aspect, traditional Christian theism may be regarded as a world-view or metaphysical system."[2] Contemporary continental philosophy is deeply antimetaphysical. But contemporary analytic philosophy is not. (Although not, as Adams points out, because contemporary analytic philosophy is naively pre-Kantian, but because it is postpositivist.) Since the analytic tradition flourishes in departments of philosophy and not in departments of religious studies, it is only to be expected that traditional theists often feel more at home in the former than in the latter.

Yet this, of course, raises other questions. What accounts for the pervasive influence of continental philosophy in religious studies departments? And why are members of religious studies departments more likely to dismiss questions of the truth of religious claims as ill-formed or inappropriate?

The essays of Stephen Crites and Philip Quinn furnish part of the answer. Religious studies departments are cross-cultural. Members of those departments are constantly exposed to the variety of human religious expression, and to the rich alternatives to theism. Furthermore, as Crites says, faculty and students in religious studies departments typically "know and care more about 'religion'" as a complex set of practices, texts, myths, social relations, psychological attitudes, and so on, than their counterparts in departments of philosophy. As a consequence, their approach to the study of religion tends to be strongly interdisciplinary. It is also significant that the methods they adopt are to a large extent those of the social sciences and of the humanities (especially of those branches of the humanities that are centrally concerned with the interpretation of texts).

If this is correct, it is fairly easy to understand why those in religious studies are so often reluctant to raise questions of truth and falsity, and why (when they are raised) they so often dismiss them as inappropriate. As Quinn points out, the social sciences as such are not concerned with the truth or adequacy of the institutions, practices, and ideological systems they investigate. A religious studies approach to religion resembles a scientific studies approach to science. The latter is not (qua scientific studies) concerned with the truth or falsity of the scientific theories it examines or, for that matter, with the epistemic value of science itself. In so far as religious studies adopts the methods of the social sciences, questions of the truth of religious claims will thus seem misplaced.[3] They are also likely to seem misplaced if one approaches religion as literature.

Constant exposure to the variety of religious practices and world-views may be even more important. Assertions of superiority on the part of theists can seem arrogant and uninformed to a person who is acquainted with the spiritual and intellectual richness and depth of such nontheistic traditions as Advaita Vedanta or Madhyamika. For she knows that arguments for theism can be paired with sophisticated arguments for different and incompatible but very attractive religious world-views. And she is also painfully aware of the difficulty of finding a neutral standpoint from which these conflicts can be adjudicated. Under these circumstances, interpretation universalism, relativism, or (at the very least) a sense of the futility of pressing questions of truth and falsity are obvious temptations.

Its association with the social sciences and humanities also helps explain another feature of philosophy of religion as practiced in religious studies departments. As Lowe and Crites point out, the social sciences and humanities concern themselves with the human subject. When the methods of the social sciences, literature, art history, and so on, are applied to the study of religion, the focus is thus likely to be upon the *subject* of religion, not its object. As a result, the philosopher will be less concerned with questions of God's existence or of the reality of the nirguna Brahman than with the question of whether the postulation of these things is (in Crites' words) "a necessary ground of personal and/or political freedom or whether it implies the radical denial of such freedom." An emphasis upon questions of freedom and justice, rather than upon questions of truth, thus becomes intelligible. The contrast with philosophy of religion as practiced in typical departments of philosophy is striking. Lowe and Crites may overstate the case when they say that analytic philosophy adopts a "scientific" model and accuse analytic philosophers of religion of applying technical reason to subject matter to which it is inappropriate (God, the Other, the religious subject). They are nevertheless on to something. Analytic philosophy *is* historically associated with science and shares science's comparative confidence in reason's ability to discover truth about its object. But the deeper explanation for these contrasts may lie in the different histories of departments of religion and departments of philosophy.

Wayne Proudfoot calls our attention to the fact that departments of religion "are offspring of faculties of Protestant theology." The aim of these faculties was "to train scholars and clergy to interpret a particular tradition in a way that makes it available for contemporary religious life," and their approach was "broadly hermeneutical." Departments of religion differ from their predecessors in typically including spokespersons for Islam, Asian religions, marginalized religious traditions, and so on. But their aim is similar —to interpret and redescribe the relevant traditions in a way that "illumines contemporary issues." And like the theologians who preceded them, their preferred genre is the "edifying discourse" addressed to "a rather broad public." Given this background it is unsurprising that AAR philosophers of religion tend to employ hermeneutical methods, address themselves to the bearing of religious traditions on issues of freedom and authenticity, and eschew scholastic niceties that would be inappropriate in an edifying discourse. Adams suggests that the interest AAR philosophers of religion have in reinterpretation may also partly explain the appeal of ambiguity, anti-realism, and interpretation universalism, For "one attraction of such...approaches is that a conservative retention of traditional credal and liturgical formulas can be combined with a more or less radical reinterpretation of their function."

APA philosophers of religion work in a quite different context. Epistemology is central to the philosophical enterprise that begins with Descartes and to the analytic tradition which inherits its concerns. Furthermore, while the western philosophical tradition as a whole is by no means indifferent to questions of edification (witness Plato, or even Hume), it has, like science, prized the search for truth for its own sake. Aristotle speaks for many philosophers in that tradition when he argues that the highest form of human activity is the expression of nous, not phronesis. And in its pursuit of truth, western philosophy has prized analytic precision and rigor of argument. (Anyone who regards the technical exactness of modern analytic philosophy as an anomaly need only re-read Plato's later dialogues, Aristotle's metaphysics, or any philosophical product of the middle ages.) It is thus natural that philosophy's preferred genre is not the edifying discourse but the tightly reasoned professional article or monograph addressed to other professional philosophers. So if this is the context in which APA philosophers of religion work, it is to be expected that they should focus on questions of the truth and rationality of religious beliefs, and pursue these questions in rigorously argued and analytically precise works largely addressed to professional philosophers and advanced students of philosophy. Nor is it surprising that, as Adams says, analytic philosophers have had little to say about the reinterpretation of traditions. (Although, in principle, there is no reason why analytic techniques couldn't be "fruitfully applied to...these issues.")

The professional context, aims, and rhetorical strategies of the two types of philosophy of religion thus differ. Yet, as Proudfoot says, this does not imply that either approach is illegitimate or unimportant. That APA and AAR philosophers of religion so often assume that the work of their counterparts *is* illegitimate or unimportant is unfortunate and should be subjected to serious critical scrutiny.

So what morals can we draw from these papers? First, as Quinn says, APA philosophers of religion should take "the affective and social dimensions of religious life" more seriously than they do, and address issues of "social construction and cultural context." Second, analytic philosophers all too often proceed as if theism were the only attractive religious option although, as Adams points out, there is no intrinsic reason why analytic tools couldn't be profitably applied to non-western doctrines and arguments.

With a few notable exceptions such as John Hick and Keith Yandell, most analytic philosophers of religion are massively ignorant of nontheistic religious traditions. They are therefore blind to their intellectual and spiritual appeal. It is hardly surprising, then, that religious relativism isn't a temptation for most of them. A deeper acquaintance with other traditions would make analytic philosophers of religion more sensitive to the difficulty (although not necessarily impossibility) of establishing the superiority of a theistic world-view. A dialogue with able and philosophically sophisticated representatives of other faiths could also enrich their perspectives on the Real (to use Hick's term) and humanity's relation to it. Finally, analytic philosophers of religion need to take the hermeneutics of suspicion seriously. I believe that Westphal is correct in saying that analytic philosophers of religion have been largely blind "to the cognitive implications of finitude and sin." As a result, they have ignored the ideological uses and abuses of theistic metaphysics and the ethical issues this raises. On this score, analytic philosophers can learn much from continental philosophy.

But the shortcomings aren't all on one side. For there are several reasons for thinking that AAR philosophers of religion should pay more attention to questions of truth and rationality than they do. In the first place, more attention should be paid to the truth and rationality of the doctrines and practices of the religions they examine. My experience at sessions of the AAR has been that questions of the truth or rational adequacy of nondualism, say, or the anatman doctrine, are seldom raised. And when they are, one is often made to feel that one's question is somehow impolite. But do we really respect the men and women whose beliefs and practices we examine if we don't take their claims to truth, and rational and spiritual superiority, seriously?

There is a further reason for paying more attention to the truth of these claims. Evans makes the important point that if theism *is* true, it deeply matters. So if theism is a "live" possibility, concern with its truth or falsity isn't parochial. (And something similar can, of course, be said of Buddhism in its various forms, of Advaita Vedanta, and so on.) Thus, if concern with theism's (or Advaita's or Theravada's) truth or rational adequacy is parochial, it can't be a live hypothesis—either because it is obviously false or because it is meaningless. What analytic philosophers of religion sometimes find frustrating is the reluctance of many of their counterparts in the AAR to defend the assumption of falsity or meaninglessness against their objections or, in some cases, to even familiarize themselves with them. (Because the arguments of analytic philosophers are occasionally somewhat technical, this reluctance may be understandable. Nevertheless, the niceties of some of these discussions are surely no harder to master than the intricacies of Hegel or Derrida.)

Second, Quinn may be right in contending that AAR philosophers of religion should adopt a more critical attitude towards the empirical adequacy of the various "social-scientific explanations of religious phenomena" that they employ. Are the theories that are used testable, for example, or supported by adequate field research?

Third, more attention should be directed towards the rational credentials of the interpretation universalism and relativism which are so often taken for granted. Doing so involves serious technical work—precisely the sort of thing analytic philosophers are good at. Many of my colleagues in the AAR greeted the appearance of Richard Rorty's *Philosophy and the Mirror of Nature* with enthusiasm. Conversations led me to believe that at least some of them had only read the third part carefully, and that the controversial and quite technical arguments which comprise the bulk of Rorty's book, and justify the conclusion he draws in part III, hadn't been examined with the same care. Is it too much to suggest that we have here a counterpart to the APA philosophers' failure to work through the findings of the social sciences, patiently and sympathetically examine non-western religious traditions, and explore the riches of continental thought?

Finally, Merold Westphal argues that some continental philosophers need to take their own "talk about openness to the other" more seriously than they do by being more open to the human otherness of fundamentalists, evangelicals, and other traditional theists, and ultimately perhaps to the divine other.

It is obvious that AAR and APA philosophers of religion have much to learn from each other. Both groups have their strengths and weaknesses. Each is too quick to notice the mote in the other's eye while overlooking the beam in its own. Philosophers from both groups are too often arrogant and parochial. But by listening to and arguing with one another one may hope that philosophers from each camp will learn to understand and appreciate their counterparts, enriching their own positions in the process.

APA and AAR philosophers of religion need each other. Let us do all we can to encourage a fruitful dialogue.

Notes

[1] However, this hostility is much less common (or, in any case, less openly expressed than when I began teaching thirty-five years ago. Part of the reason may be a feature of analytic philosophy as currently practiced to which Wolterstorff calls our attention. Analytic philosophy has, by and large, rejected classical foundationalism without adopting interpretation universalism. It has instead embraced what he calls "unabashedly ungrounded perspectival particularism" —the denial that we must show that our starting points are "more probable than not on the available evidence of certitudes." The rejection of classical foundationalism and adoption of ungrounded particularism has created a climate in which one can as easily take traditional theism as one's starting point as, say, physicalism.

[2] Basil Mitchell, *The Justification of Religious Belief* (London: Macmillan, 1973), page 99.

[3] As Quinn says, religious studies' association with the social sciences also helps explain its affinity for continental philosophy. For the classics of social studies have their roots in that tradition. That departments of religion are heirs of departments of theology is also undoubtedly a factor. For the theological classics of the last two centuries, too, grow out of that tradition.

1

Between the Pincers of Increased Diversity and Supposed Irrationality

Nicholas Wolterstorff

The question for consideration is why it is that philosophers of religion primarily associated with the American Philosophical Association tend either to exhibit in their thinking that they are themselves traditional theists or to take only traditional theism seriously, whereas neither of these is the case for philosophers of religion primarily associated with the American Academy of Religion. Of course the question begs the thesis that this is how things are. My own evidence, though entirely anecdotal, all points toward the conclusion that it is.

Let me first remark that though I think it has been true for a long time that philosophers primarily associated with the APA tend either to exhibit in their thinking that they are traditional theists or to take only traditional theism seriously, it is also my clear impression that in recent years there has been a dramatic shift of proportions as between the two sides of that disjunction. The number of those whose work exhibits traditional theism has increased dramatically *vis a vis* those who only take it seriously. It has been true for a long time now that members of the guild of the APA, when doing philosophy of religion, tended to be interested only in traditional theism. But when I entered the guild of the APA, more than thirty years ago, what little philosophy of religion there was not only tended to focus entirely on traditional theism but to be either hostile toward it or professedly neutral. Those were the postures acceptable among philosophers. The only significant exception that comes to mind was O. K. Bouwsma. What has happened over the past twenty years is that, as it were, the Bouwsmas have become legion—though I should immediately add that no one has yet turned up capable of matching Bouwsma in wit and irony! I don't know whether the membership of the APA now contains a higher proportion of traditional theists than it did some thirty years ago; but whether it does or not, the important and truly remarkable development, so I suggest, is that the traditional theists have come out of the closet. If that's right, then the question is why that happened.

Let me hold that question for a while and turn to the other side of the matter. When we talk about philosophers of religion primarily associated with the AAR, we are talking—at least I'll assume we are talking—about philosophers who are for the most part located in religious studies departments. What follows is going to be some history which is in good measure, though not entirely, arm-chair history.

Religious studies departments are a recent development; they don't belong to the natural order of things in academia. I would guess that few emerged before the second world war. So we have to ask why they emerged. And I think the basic story to be told here is that told by George Marsden in his recent *The Soul of the American University*. My own version of the story goes as follows.

The American polity, from its very beginnings as an *American* polity in contrast to a collection of colonial polities, was faced with the issue of how a diversity of religious visions and communities could live together in peace within a single polity. In principle there are various answers to that question. And not only in principle: if one looks about in space and history, one sees a variety of different answers in operation. At the founding of our own nation, however, there wasn't really any doubt as to what our answer would be. So much had our founding fathers been shaped by the thought of John Locke that the only answer they considered was the liberal answer.

Fundamental to the liberal solution is the distinction between the private sphere and the public. How exactly that distinction is drawn can and does differ a good deal from time to time within a given society and from one society to another; some such distinction, however, is indispensable. Always of course the state belongs to the public sphere; almost always a good deal of the educational system belongs as well, and a bit of the economy. The liberal proposes, then, that for life within the public sphere the citizens not use as their source of legitimation and orientation any of the traditions represented by the competing religions and visions of the good, but that they appeal to something independent of all those. The yield of this source must be sufficient to legitimate and orient actions within the public sphere—in particular, actions within the political sphere and within the academic. And it must in addition be a source whose deliverances everyone ought to acknowledge; it must in that way be neutral. Whether everyone does in fact acknowledge its deliverances is another matter. It's characteristic of liberals to be paternalistically hortatory, even threatening, in their treatment of the views of those who dissent from the liberal dream; Locke already provided an example of that in his treatment of the Enthusiasts.

What is that source? Again, a number of possibilities suggest themselves, abstractly considered. There are nowadays a number of polities, sprinkled around the globe, which appear to think that a shared nationalism will do the trick. But we all know the answer that Locke and all his followers gave: Reason is that source. Our common life—particularly our political and academic life—is to be based on Reason—supplemented, indeed, with experience.

It's important for our purposes to add that Locke did not regard his insistence, that in the public sphere we appeal solely to Reason and not to the deliverances of our several traditions, as implying the removal of all religious conviction from the public sphere; he would have been disturbed if he had thought it did imply that. Though he believed that there is a good deal in religion that is irrational, he most emphatically did not believe that all of it is that. He believed, and in his day he was far from alone in believing, that listening to "the voice of Reason" yields a sizeable body of religious conviction within both "natural" and "revealed" religion. He wrote of *The Reasonableness of Christianity*. I submit that one of the dynamics behind the emergence of religious studies departments is the steady erosion within our liberal polity of the conviction that Christianity—or any other form of traditional theism—is in fact rational.

Let me elaborate a bit. The liberal experiment which we have been trying out here in America says that our public academies must be neutral as among the competing religions; and though every now and then we grab fragments of our supposedly-shared nationalism and import them into the schools without wondering about the rationality of it all, mainly we have thought that the way to make them neutral without consigning them to silence is to insist that they base what they do on Reason and experience. In this situation, two dynamics have emerged and come together like a powerful pincers to produce our religious studies departments. One is the dynamic just mentioned: the spread of skepticism concerning the rationality of religion, especially of Christianity, but more generally, of theism. Already in the eighteenth century many thinkers dumped so-called "revealed religion" into the dustbin of irrationality; in our century, many have tossed so-called natural religion in with revealed. The other dynamic is the radical expansion of religious diversity since the founding of our country, and the emboldening of various members of that expanded diversity to remark that the academy as it actually conducts itself does not appear to them the least bit neutral. Catholics began saying that the academy appeared to them Protestant; Jews began saying that the academy appeared to them Christian; adherents of Eastern religions began saying that the academy appeared to them theist; and atheists began saying that the academy appeared to them religious.

I think there can be little doubt that the emergence of religious studies departments after the second world war was the result of the pincers of which these two dynamics were the arms. For a university in the public domain to espouse any particular religion—not just traditional theism, but any particular religion—would be to violate the fundamental standards of rationality operative in the academy, and to forsake the neutrality required by it on the liberal model. Of course that doesn't imply that private universities cannot espouse some particular religion; but as Marsden shows, the pressure on a private university which wants to be of national significance to act like a public university has been, in most cases, irresistible. It also doesn't straightforwardly imply that individual faculty members within a public university cannot espouse their own religion. To allow them to do that within the university would be to opt for the *consociational* model for dealing with religious diversity, rather than the *liberal* model. As a matter of fact, my own university, Yale, has basically opted for that model in structuring its religious studies department. But I submit that the liberal model for handling religious diversity has been so deeply ingrained in most Americans that the emergence of religious studies departments in which all the members are expected to place their religious commitments on the shelf was all but inevitable—especially in the public universities.

By around the middle of our century, then, the espousal of religion within the university was regarded as out of bounds. University chapels and chaplains, university theologians—they all had to go. Yet religion is too important a part of human life for a university simply to ignore it. So what to do? Well, institute a department whose business it is to *teach about* religion rather than espouse it; that would satisfy both the canons of rationality and the requirements of neutrality. Remember that the U.S. Supreme Court was enjoining the same stance on the public lower schools at roughly the same time. Teach about religion in its various forms. If you believe that religion has an *essence* of which those various forms are the *manifestations,* then teach that essence too. And teach courses in which the question considered is whether or not there is an essence. It helped a lot that phenomenology of religion appeared on the scene at just this time. But see to it that *nobody espouses* either religion as such, or any version thereof; to espouse either religion in general or some religion in particular would be to violate both the academic canons of rationality and the social requirement of neutrality. Karl Barth would not have candidated for a position in a religious studies department!

Let me now return to the question I posed concerning those who do their work within the guild of the APA. What is it that accounts for the dramatic increase there in the number of those philosophers of religion—and philosophers generally—who make no attempt whatsoever to conceal their adherence to one or another form of traditional theism? I submit that the clue, in this case, is the rejection of classically modern foundationalism within the philosophical academy. Or more precisely, the clue is a particular *kind* of such rejection.

Classically modern foundationalism is rejected on all fronts today. It would take more courage than most intellectuals possess to stand up today and say loudly: "Yes, I'm a classical foundationalist; and so what?" The accusation of being a classical foundationalist has a chilling effect in the academy rather like the accusation of being a child molester in general society. The important point for my purposes here, however, is that there have been two quite different fronts of rejection, focussed on different aspects of that complex phenomenon which is foundationalism of the classically modern sort.

Part and parcel of classically modern foundationalism was a representational picture of the mind, of a pre-Kantian sort. The picture was that each of us is aware of his or her own present mental states, objects, and acts; they are present to us. Beyond that, however, presence, and one's awareness of what is present, does not extend. But as luck would have it—or divine creation, or evolution—among the mental objects of which we are aware are images which are representations of remembered events in the past, and others which are representations of perceived external objects. By way of these representations we are able to get a cognitive grip on the past and the external; and in turn, by way of inferences from beliefs about these—beliefs which are *certain* because they are just "read off" from what is presented to us—we can form well-grounded beliefs about the past and about the external.

One front of rejection of classically modern foundationalism focuses on this pre-Kantian representational picture of the mind, and rejects it on the ground that we don't have even that tiny bit of awareness which the traditional representationalist affirmed. Reality is never anywhere present to us—not even our own present mental reality. In experience, representation is all, in inner sense as well as outer. But not representation as the pre-Kantians understood it, as *images;* but representation as Kant understood it, as always-already-conceptualized experience-stuff—for which a better model than reflective images is representational paintings. To peel away the interpretation from the interpreted experience would not be to get at the pure given but to lose the only given we have—the interpreted given. Prisoners, all of us, within the house of interpretation.

But further: Why suppose that beyond our shot-through-with-interpretation experience there is a ready-made structured world, hanging around, waiting for us to interpret it? Is the supposition even intelligible? Any attempt to think such a world will already be an interpretation of it, a conceptualizing of it. Better to conclude that things exist, and are as they are, only relative to one or another of our conceptual schemes. Of course there's more than our conceptual schemes. But that more—unless one is speaking within some conceptual scheme—is just primeval Ur-stuff whose only character as such is susceptibility to our interpretations. Though one must not think of it as coming *ready-made* bearing the property of susceptibility to interpretations—for to think of it as susceptible to interpretations is also to interpret it. Formless chaos, whose only character as such is susceptibility to the imposition of form. And it doesn't even come *ready-made* bearing the property of susceptibility to the imposition of form—for to think of it as susceptible to the imposition of form is to interpret it as having that much form. Hard to think!

This, I say, is one front of rejection of classical foundationalism: Call it *interpretation-universalism,* blended, typically, with metaphysical anti-realism. It's the fashionable view throughout most of North Atlantic academia—including, so far as I can tell, American religious studies departments. Very often the image of being human which accompanies this fashionable view is that to be human is to seek to gain power over the other and to resist the attempt of the other likewise to gain power. Those in religious studies departments who work with that image see themselves as having an additional motive for resisting, if not theism in general, at least traditional Christian theism: Christianity is an intrinsic component within that old hegemony of power which has to be overturned. An Old Order Amish person, a Hasidic Jew—they might be tolerated, since they never were part of the hegemonic consensus and carry little threat of ever becoming so. Presbyterians—they're quite a different matter.

There remain some pockets of unfashionability, however. Philosophers of a generally analytic orientation constitute one such. Yes, I know that we have our Putnams, our Rortys, and our Goodmans. But they're the exception. The front of rejection most common among philosophers of a generally analytic orientation focuses on quite a different aspect of classically modern foundationalism from that mentioned above. Not that most such philosophers would actually defend that old representational picture of the mind; they wouldn't. But the number who reject it by espousing interpretation-universalism and metaphysical anti-realism is relatively few. What analytic philosophers typically reject in classically modern foundationalism are the claims made as to how we ought to conduct our understandings or as to what constitutes knowledge. And the analytic philosopher, rightly or wrongly, hasn't thought that he had to get into issues concerning the nature of the understanding in order to criticize those claims. His argument is that it's just not true that our beliefs about external objects, and about the past, and even about God, lack warrant, or entitlement, or justification—you name it—unless they are based on beliefs of ours which are supposedly certain because they are just "read off" from mental facts present to the mind.

The result of this rejection, among philosophers of a generally analytic orientation, has been what I think can best be thought of as unabashedly ungrounded *perspectival particularism.* It's not at all unusual nowadays for philosophers who call themselves "physicalists" to unabashedly begin a paper by announcing that they wish to explore one or another aspect of physicalism—without on that occasion or any other making a pretense of establishing that physicalism is more probable than not on the available evidence of certitudes. And likewise, it is becoming less and less unusual for philosophers who regard themselves as theists of one form or another to act similarly. The physicalist assumes that he is not irrational in being a physicalist; the theist, that he is not irrational in being a theist. My thesis is that the emergence of a sizeable number of philosophers who unabashedly take some form of traditional theism as their philosophical orientation—both within philosophy of religion and beyond—is part of this remarkable emergence within contemporary analytic philosophy of unabashedly ungrounded perspectival particularism. It's post-Locke, of course, but also post-Kant: That's the clue.

Yes, I said it right: post-Kant. It really is possible to be post-Kantian. It's possible to recover from Kant. The choices are not exhausted between being naively pre-Kantian, on the one hand, and being a Kantian of one or another stripe, on the other. Those who have most enraptured contemporary academia with their narratives of contemporary philosophy have talked as if all the waters of philosophy rushed down just one channel after the dam of classically modern foundationalism broke: Down the channel of interpretation-universalism and metaphysical anti-realism. But they didn't all rush down one channel. Philosophy after foundationalism has gone down two very different channels. And one of those channels is post-Kantian as much as it is post-foundationalist. The philosophers who swim in this channel—to change my metaphor slightly—are not naively uninformed. They are fully aware of interpretation-universalism and fully aware of metaphysical anti-realism; but after serious consideration, they have rejected these options as untenable. Those unaware of this development are the ones who are outdated in their thinking, not up to date.

The philosophers of religion who mainly work within the guild of the APA are almost all post-foundationalists of the post-Kantian sort. It's my impression that those who mainly work within religious studies departments and the guild of the AAR are almost all post-foundationalists of a Kantian sort.

That completes my attempt to account for our present situation. What of the future? Well, the widespread rejection of classically modern foundationalism and of everything similar thereto has, in my judgment, removed the intellectual underpinnings from the liberal solution to the challenge of religiously diverse communities existing within one polity. Epistemology has social consequences. I think that leaves us with no choice but to go in the direction of social pluralism—the consociational solution. And as to metaphysics and epistemology, my own guess is that the anti-realist, interpretation-universalist branch of post-foundationalism will shortly dry up, principally, I would guess, because of its self-referential incoherence and its inability to answer the charge of moral relativism.

2

Traditional Theism, the AAR, and the APA

Merold Westphal

It seems to me that there does tend to be the suggested difference between philosophers of religion in the APA and those in the AAR. Why this is the case I do not profess to know. I have some ideas, which I am about to share with you, but I am not very confident that they go very far to explain the phenomenon in question. I hope my colleagues will have on this topic, as they regularly do on others, better insight than mine. I shall restrict my scope to Christian theism both 1) because I think most of those involved relate, positively or negatively, to this tradition more than to any other and 2) because I don't think I understand the situation of Jewish scholars, for example, well enough to say anything about it.

My first suggestion has to do with the fragile place of Religious Studies in the American university. This is a special case of the larger phenomenon that might be called the secularization of the American university, recently studied in some detail by George Marsden and Stephen Carter. Many American intellectuals have a basically allergic reaction in the face of religious ideas and practices, and the institutionalizing of anything having to do with religion within the academy makes them very nervous. Against the background of the Enlightenment affirmation of the autonomy of the intellect and, more specifically, the tension between religion and science associated with the names of Galileo and Darwin there has developed during the twentieth century a relation of mutual distrust and deep suspicion between secular intellectuals and Christians of a conservative theological orientation, whether they be fundamentalists, evangelicals, or simply confessionally orthodox Catholics or Protestants (all of whom, it should be noted, are traditional theists as I understand the term to be used in the present context).

In my view, which I commend to you as indisputably and incontrovertibly, well, mine, this attitude of mutual hostility is partly an irrational prejudice on the part of each party, and, just for that reason, partly a justifiable reaction to the narrow mindedness of the other side. But regardless of the degree to which these mutual suspicions are justified or not, they are (and have been) a fact that only further complicates the status of Religious Studies programs. I say further because in public universities questions of church and state already make the establishment of Religious Studies programs a delicate matter, while in private universities that wish to cultivate a broad, nonsectarian clientele something of the same dynamics is at work. (And these two types of university dominate the field of large and prestigious universities whose graduate programs will largely staff Religious Studies programs both in such universities and in smaller, liberal arts colleges.) When, in addition to these factors, there is on the part of secular intellectuals who play no small part in American university life, a deep distrust of religious ideas and practices, the establishment and maintenance of Religious Studies programs will be a different sort of enterprise from that of other programs.

Some, like Richard Rorty, have the integrity of being quite candid and up front about their perceptions of religion and the academy as antithetical. But this openness has the serious disadvantage that when one explicitly articulates the perceived incompatibility of religious commitment and intellectual life, the position can be examined and debated. For Rorty, who has the courage of his convictions about conversation, this is not a disadvantage. But I fear that for many others it is; it is simply easier to have this incompatibility something that everyone knows but no one discusses.

For a long time colleges and universities with strong church relations or nondenominational schools with a strong religious identity have had departments of Biblical Studies and of Theology. I do not know just when or how it came to be thought that other types of institution should have departments of Religious Studies, but it is a relatively recent development, and it has taken place in the context I have been trying to describe. The prevailing consensus has not been that such programs should be staffed by those hostile to religion as such, but rather that they should be staffed by those whose positive appreciation of the religious dimension of life is as safe as possible, least likely to offend the prevailing ethos in the academy (which, in my view, is a mixture of legitimate and illegitimate elements).

I think it is possible to give a fairly workable working definition to this notion of safety. To be safe is to stay away from the conservative end of the theological spectrum. As one moves from right to left along that spectrum, from fundamentalists, to evangelicals, to the confessionally orthodox, the first folks one meets are traditional theists. As one moves further left one encounters liberal Christians (both Catholic and Protestant) for whom various aspects of traditional theism have fallen by the wayside and, beyond that, various forms of pluralism and pantheism whose theistic commitments range from negligible to nonexistent. In this context there is a tendency, not absolute, but strong, toward the mutual exclusivity of safety and theism.

I think it is becoming increasingly clear that this situation is highly problematic for these two reasons (among others): first, in spite of its professed commitment to pluralism, the academy becomes far more exclusionary than its legitimate concern for open and rational conversation requires; and second, a false sense of security *vis-a-vis* the issue of indoctrination is engendered. For the positions perceived as safe are quite capable of the dogmatic exclusion of their opposites and of creating an atmosphere of political correctness that discourages (if that is not too weak a term) open discussion. Dogmatic pluralism, for example, or dogmatic feminism, can be forms of fundamentalism. Thus I, for one, welcome the new and growing discussion of such issues as the relation of religion to the academy and the relation of advocacy to teaching.

Although Philosophy departments live in the same world that Religious Studies departments live in, it does not seem to me that the dynamics I have been discussing have affected them in anything like the same degree, and this for several reasons:

1) The discipline as a whole does not make people nervous in the same way that the study of religion does. It does not raise problems of church and state, and, alas, it has been perceived for a long time as quintessentially safe by virtue of its irrelevance to life outside its own bailiwick; and, insofar as it has more recently begun to look quite dangerous indeed to some people, the threat of the nihilistic French and their wild American disciples has been overwhelmingly staffed by those whose secularism is conspicuous. As one friend of mine has put it, Derrida doesn't have a religious bone in his body.

2) There is a long-standing tradition that philosophy of religion is a legitimate subdivision of the discipline, one that does not engender the same nervousness as do Religious Studies departments in the university for several reasons. a) It is somewhat peripheral. It is like aesthetics in the sense that a university could have a prestigious program without having any senior person who covers that field. Thus it is more nearly accidental than essential to the discipline. b) Those who do philosophy of religion can and often do work in other areas, historical and/or problem oriented, that are perceived to be more or less religiously neutral. They can thus prove that they really are philosophers, that they belong in the academy, in this "neutral" territory. c) Much of the subject matter of the philosophy of religion turns out to be pretty safe, after all. Debates over divine simplicity or

middle knowledge, or even over the existence of God *vis-a-vis* the evil in the world are easily perceived as quite distant from discourse about the God who makes claims on people's lives and makes many in the academy nervous. The**ists** are relatively harmless because the**ism** is (perceived as) relatively innocuous. For these and doubtless other reasons, the philosophy of religion division of the philosophical discipline has felt less threatened by those with theistic commitments and thus more open to them than departments of Religious Studies.

I do not mean to suggest that Philosophy is immune to anti-religious bias. I have experienced it myself on more than one occasion. Both as a graduate student and as a junior faculty member I found Yale to be a genuinely open institution. My religious identity, which I neither flaunted nor tried to disguise, was not held against me even by those whom it clearly made nervous. Unfortunately, I have not always found that same spirit elsewhere. There may well be some Philosophy departments even more adamantly closed to those with theistic convictions than any Religious Studies department. But this seems to me to be more a local matter in the former case whereas it may be more a systemic matter in the latter.

My second suggestion is the observation that among philosophers of religion the AAR/APA division tends to correspond with a continental philosophy/analytic philosophy division. I do not take this latter distinction to be either in fact or in current perception anything like as clean an either/or as it once seemed to many to be. But just as the differences between East and West Germany did not simply disappear when the Berlin wall came down, so there remain real differences between continental and analytic philosophy even while the iron curtain between them has been melting.

I hasten to add that I do not think this difference really explains the difference we are trying to explain. I do not think that people first become philosophers of a certain sort and then on that basis take up a position on the theological spectrum. I think the relation is much more complex and more nearly circular. But I cannot escape the sense that if we wish to understand the theological difference that has been put before us we cannot ignore this philosophical difference.

I return to the distinction drawn above between the**ists** and the**ism**. By the**ism** I understand a fairly well defined, traditional body of propositional claims about the existence and nature of a personal God. There is no necessity, either in fact or in logic, that a philosopher of religion who is a the**ist** should take as his or her primary task the articulation and defense of the**ism**.

(I give myself as an example of one who does not.) But it is natural that some, even many, would make this their primary task, and I think it is clear that analytic philosophy lends itself to this debate in ways that continental philosophy does not. One slightly tendentious way to put this would be to say that much analytic philosophy of religion is stubbornly pre-Kantian,[1] whereas continental philosophy is systematically post-Kantian. For this reason analytic philosophy provides a friendlier context for the articulation and defense of theism than continental philosophy does. The natural home for theists with this project is philosophy departments with an analytic orientation.

There is work for theistic philosophers to do on the continental slopes of the academic vineyard, but fewer have found it. On the one hand it consists in reiterating the Kantian dictum that the denial of knowledge makes room for faith. Secular continentalists often develop powerful arguments for the claim that we do not have Absolute Knowledge of anything, most especially of anything Absolute, like the God of traditional theism. But they often talk as if they had shown that there is nothing Absolute, like the God of traditional theism. They normally leave this "argument" sufficiently implicit that its *non sequiturial* character does not get noticed. Someone needs to point out 1) that the argument, so far as it has any plausibility, has been an epistemological argument about our incapacity to realize certain Platonic, Cartesian, Hegelian ideals of cognition, and 2) that without the dogmatic claim that our knowledge is the criterion of what there is it is neutral about what may be the case ontologically. The onto-theo-logical project may be a form of human hybris, but so is the claim that to show this is to show that theistic beliefs are false, that there is no God who is in fact the ground and the unity of all being.

On the other hand there is the task of showing the religious value and importance, even or especially for theists, in qualifying our God talk, whether philosophical or theological, with the kind of attention to the cognitive implications of finitude and sin that is typical of continental philosophy.

In other words, we may be about due for the kind of change in continental philosophy that has already taken place in analytic philosophy. There was a time when the latter was perceived to be a safely secular domain. That has changed quite dramatically in the last couple of decades. At present the continental scene is dominated by secularism and what might be called from a religious point of view the thinnest of theological soups. But that might change. Brave talk about Openness to the Other may come home to roost, and the tendency toward the exclusion of theistic discourses may dissipate, either gradually or quite suddenly. If that happens, the differences between the AAR and the APA may begin to dissipate as well.

Notes

[1] In response to the suggestion that philosophical theology in the analytic tradition often tends to be pre-Kantian, my good friend Nick Wolterstorff once responded something like this. "Do not think that we are naively pre-Kantian. We know all about Kant; we just don't accept his point of view. Kant is not a terminal disease. It is possible to get over him." I promised that in order to avoid any possible implication of naiveté, I would henceforth speak of those who are **stubbornly** pre-Kantian. I am here keeping that promise.

3

Two Types of Philosophy of Religion

Walter Lowe

As my experience is much more with the AAR than with the APA, my homework in preparation for this discussion was to spend some quiet afternoons paging through back issues of three journals which I had previously tended simply to dip into, namely *Religious Studies*, *The International Journal for Philosophy of Religion* and *Faith and Philosophy*. Others can comment on how precisely these publications reflect what goes on in the APA; my impression is that there is an affinity. In any event, two things seem clear. Among the journals themselves there is a family resemblance. And that family is of a different tribe from what frequently, though not always, appears under the heading of philosophy of religion in the AAR.

In the essay from which I have cribbed my title, Paul Tillich distinguishes between an "ontological" and a "cosmological" approach.[1] While not rejecting the latter out of hand, Tillich is clear that the cosmological must ever be secondary to, and derivative of, an existential awareness which is the defining mark of the ontological. For otherwise the cosmological winds up with an ultimate being, and thus with God as a being among other beings: a conclusion which Tillich famously decries.

So one way of giving content to the term "theism" would be to identify it, as Tillich does, with the dubious practice of regarding God as a being among other beings. But if that is what is meant by "theism," then it seems to me that the term is not adequate to either the variety or the subtlety that one finds in the journals in question. As prima facie evidence, consider the extraordinary frequency of reference to Soren Kierkegaard, who is the touchstone for much of what is meant by "existential awareness": a computer search indicates that in back issues of the three journals there are one hundred and forty-two treating Kierkegaard in some way. Turning from Tillich, we might seek instruction from Jurgen Moltmann, who understands theism to be implacably wedded to the notion of divine immutability. But here too, what the term gains in clarity, it loses in applicability to the periodicals.

Prompted by these misgivings, I shall propose a typology which is different from those of Tillich and Moltmann, though it can be discerned somewhat below the surface in the Tillich essay. Of the power of Being Tillich says that "it is the *point of identity* without which neither separation not interaction can be thought."[2] But he also says that it "is the power *of everything that has power*, be it a universal or an individual, a thing or an experience."[3] Tillich himself, of course, was intent upon holding these two perspectives together. Shuttling between polyphonic experience and unitary ground provides the dynamic of much of his thought. But considered independently of Tillich's project, the two formulations do point in different directions; they echo the classic agon of the One and the Many. And the first vector, namely the pursuit of an ultimate "point of identity," does seem a fairly accurate, unprejudicial description of most of what I read those fall afternoons. As for the other tribe more indigenous to the AAR—might we not think of it as a more pluralistic, phenomenological exploration of every possible site or sighting of sacred power?

We have, in any case, the beginnings of a typology. Let us call the two approaches "T" and "non-T" respectively, or the "first" and "second" type. As to the purpose of the typology, I will offer occasional asides about applicability and sociology, but my primary interest will be in the *logic* of the types: their points of convergence and the possible reasons for conflict between them.

As a first step in exploring the logic, we may note in the journals under consideration a frequent appeal to formal logic. More generally, we find in them a mode of argument which is more or less deliberately cast along the lines of data, warrant, backing and conclusion, to use the language of Stephen Toulmin.[4] (This is something different than to say that the arguments *could* be so articulated; that would be true of most any intelligible argument.) The argument is expressly articulated along these general lines; and its ability to be so articulated is taken to be important evidence of its tenability.

The stance toward a formal or semi-formal mode of argument is indeed a touchstone for distinguishing the two types. In the eyes of non-T, such practices are too closely allied with the world-view of the natural sciences and are questionable, at best, in treating religion. This divergence in the assessment of the natural sciences is significant. For it isn't simply that such appeals happen to occur less often in the second type. Rather, they are actively mistrusted. The reason for this mistrust seems to lie with some form of the Diltheyan distinction between explanation and understanding. Evidence for this is the fact that mirroring the presence of *formalization* in the first set of journals and its relative absence in the second, is the presence of one or another form of *hermeneutics* in the second set of writings, and the relative absence of such hermeneutics (let us say specifically Continental hermeneutics) in the first.

This is not to say that non-T takes the role of the sciences less seriously than T (though the often anthropocentric orientation of non-T might give that impression.) Non-T is fully aware of the preeminence of science in western culture; it may even exaggerate the influence. The difference lies rather at the point of assessment. To generalize, T sees science, particularly the natural sciences, as a legitimate *mode of knowledge*, irreducibly necessary though not all-sufficient. Thus T will incorporate scientific findings and consult scientific method. Non-T, for its part, tends to identify science with technical reason, a negative term, and thus to conceive it as being, in practice if not in principle, an unreflective reductionism. Far from incorporating aspects of the scientific world-view, non-T characteristically presses for an alternative to it.

We first postulated T in connection with the impetus toward an ultimate point of unity. A search for unity is consistent with a strategy of incorporation vis-a-vis science. Conversely (and this is my particular point) hermeneutical methods have tended since the time of Dilthey to forego unity in favor of a dividing of the turf. It has tended to cede a certain terrain to the natural sciences and then to set off in search of "something more." Once located and expounded, the "something more" may be claimed, indeed it almost certainly *will* be claimed—to be more basic and more originative than the mode of knowing associated with science. It will be the root of science itself. But generative kinship is no sooner proclaimed that it is put aside, largely because the offspring is regarded as backward: science is the product of narrowing and exclusion, it is specialization become fixation. One need only recall how Heidegger regards technology. Science as idiot savant may have some selective usefulness, but for non-T it is devoid of authority. Those who find in it the very spirit of alienation will leave it to its arid terrain.

This matters because suspicion of anything suggesting a unification of knowledge is apt to produce (though in deft hands it does not have to produce) a reticence about any ultimate point of unity. Regarding such a point, non-T tends to be functionally agnostic; it is far more oriented to the particularities of experience or praxis. Where it is acknowledged at all, the point of unity does not actually function as an indispensable point of reference.

Non-T thus evinces more interest in religion than in God; which is perhaps unsurprising in an academy of religion. But with God relegated to an ancillary role, questions do arise regarding the justification of religion, or the study thereof. The historian of religion or the sociologist of religion have sufficient justification in the simple fact that religion exists, that it is a phenomenon of culture. But what justification has the philosopher of religion, if the philosopher be non-T?

To ask the same question from another angle: It is obvious that T seeks unity because such a point, if affirmed, provides a conceptual resting place. Reason confirms in its peculiar fashion that "our hearts are restless until they rest in Thee." But what of non-T? Is there not some point, whether ultimate or not, where its argument comes at least provisionally to rest? I think that there is and that it occurs at that juncture or argument or exposition where non-T succeeds in affirming some significant link between religion (i.e. authentic religion), on the one hand, and *the ethical* (i.e. the truly ethical), on the other hand.

Religion deepens the ethical; the ethical validates religion. That, I submit, is the heart beat of non-T. Examples would include much reflection which proceeds under the heading of "liberation" and much which seeks to represent various marginalized voices. A *press toward the ethical* (in counterpoint to the press toward unity), and more specifically a press toward the praxiological empowerment of the ethical, functions for non-T as the crucial philosophic test within religion. Conversely any type T *press toward unity* will be confronted by non-T with such questions as "Whose unity? Unity in what interest?" Dramatic examples can be drawn from the followers of Foucault and Derrida, for whom the disavowal of unity is programmatic—and where some form of ethical concern, though less apparent, is almost always at work.

But the paradigm case, in my experience, has to do with one specific figure. Over the course of some twelve years I have been involved with organizing and maintaining two groups in the AAR which have been explicitly concerned with a sort of philosophic reflection which does *not* proceed in the formalizing mode. These have been a group on "Theology and the Phenomenological Movement" and, currently, a more broadly conceived group on "Theology and Continental Philosophy." Year by year these groups confronted the familiar task of determining what sort of issue would elicit papers. What would draw the group together? Social liberation was one broad answer; postmodernism was another. But what provoked the most emphatic and enduring response was the work of a single thinker, Emmanuel Levinas.

Not that there was a convergence of unquestioning disciples. We all had our reservations. But there was something in the Levinasian vision which we found uniquely compelling. On reflection that "something" had to do with two elements: a highly thematized critique of every conceivable press toward unity, here called "totality"; and an equally emphatic insistence upon the ethical, as made present in "the face." In Levinas these two reverberant elements are intensified to a degree which, in philosophy, is virtually without precedent. Levinas is paradigmatically non-T.

Where, then, does the paradigm point us? Levinas's indictment is sweeping and intransigent. It would nullify virtually all of western metaphysics and, it would seem, most of western culture as well. His categorical judgments make Levinas antipodal to the judicious, analytic temper of T. They signal his affinity with what Ricoeur has called the hermeneutic of suspicion. In this cause he joins hands with various liberationists and deconstructionists. So this is where the paradigm directs us: away from the affirmative atmosphere of hermeneutics at large and into suspicion's hard light. And what is suggested by this logic is confirmed by the journals. One finds in them remarkably little discussion of those clamorous voices— Marx, Nietzsche and Freud, to say nothing of black, feminist, womanist, gay and lesbian critiques—which, to judge from discussions in the AAR, define the religious agenda of our time. A computer search found five articles touching upon Freud, two on Marx and five on Nietzsche in all the published issues of the three journals combined.

In my remaining reflections I will foreground this cathected topic of suspicion. For regarding the types, it signals not just contrast but polarization; it is the most likely occasion of mutual recrimination. In an effort to mediate this stand off, I propose, if you will permit me, to introduce yet another typology. Ultimately it should mesh with T and non-T; and to avoid confusion with that typology, I will call it a schema. It has to do with various ways of understanding what Freud is about. [5]

Half the problem with psychoanalysis has always been getting clear on the exact extent of the truth claims made in its name. In brief, schematic fashion, there are four possibilities. It may be said that (1) psychoanalysis claims to say everything about everything; (2) more modestly, it claims to say everything about something; (3) more modestly still, it claims to say something about something; and (4) finally and most intriguingly, it claims to say something about everything.

"Everything about everything" is the classic formulation of reductionism. Freud says that everything is sex, everything is phallic symbol or vaginal symbol —*tertium non datur*—and if you voice reservations, that is sure sign of your own resistance. Freudianism thus appears as a closed, self-referencing system, a sort of metaphysic. Either one buys the whole program, at the price of intellectual capitulation, or one retains one's common sense and dismisses it altogether.

In contrast, the "everything about something" reading sees psychoanalysis as more circumspect. Every science has its proper object; Freud's achievement was to have brought to light a hitherto unrecognized object, namely the unconscious. Obviously the unconscious is not everything, but it *is* something, and we in the twentieth century would be very foolish to deny it altogether. Often this second approach is cast in the same language of hierarchy: what Freud says holds true for certain lower aspects of human experience, but there are other, higher aspects as well, which cannot be explained away.

The third approach, "something about something," is an extension of the second. Once again the unconscious is acknowledged as legitimate object or area of study, but now questions are raised as to the founder's adequacy even there. Freud is regarded as a sort of Columbus, for having set foot upon a new world, but also for having misnamed it and misconstrued it. He was led astray, it is often said, by the Helmholtzian physics of his day. The antidote is an alternative hermeneutic, such as the existentialist or the Jungian.

What is striking in our account of the three approaches is how closely linked are the ways of defining Freud and the ways of responding to him. The moment you cast psychoanalysis in any one of these ways, the rest of the discussion seems foreordained. In the first case, it is simply a matter of dismissing the entire enterprise, perhaps by humor and irony, perhaps by turning it upon itself. In the second and third cases, it is a matter of exploiting the fact that psychoanalysis has been defined, in the root sense of the word: limits have been set to its validity. Attention quickly shifts to other matters.

These three assessments of psychoanalysis I would associate variously with T. Together they do much to explain why psychoanalysis, and the hermeneutic of suspicion generally, are in the eyes of T of less than epochal significance. In this light, it is important to observe the distinctiveness of the final, fourth position, "something about everything." It does not portray psychoanalysis as mandating total control of the conceptual terrain; yet neither does it delimit a priori the conceptual space within which, or about which, psychoanalysis is allowed to speak. Psychoanalysis would not purport to exhaust any particular; but it is the nature of the unconscious to know no boundary, and thus each and every particular without exception would be fair game. In principle this is a perfectly logical way of understanding suspicion, yet it is difficult to place on a conventional conceptual map. Vexacious conceptually, suspicion on this account would be vexacious in more palpable ways as well. Without making the overweening (and vulnerable) truth claims characteristic of an absolute reductionism, psychoanalysis would nevertheless seem reductionistic. After all, for the person on the receiving end, a psychoanalysis which proposed to say "something about everything" might very well *feel like* it were claiming to say "everything about everything." There is the peculiar insistence; the suspicion is always there, presuming to speak on the momentous and trivial alike. There is no way of de-fining it, no way of setting limits; no way of securing for oneself a safe and privileged place.

My notion has been to address our "why" question—why are there these differences in philosophy of religion?—not by looking for socio-political causes, important as those are, but rather by exploring the internal logic of two possibly pertinent types. In concluding I will not review what has been said about the press toward a point of unity and about hermeneutics. That contrast may be sufficiently recalled by noting how unlikely it is that one would encounter a hermeneutical argument for the existence of God. Rather I shall close by suggesting that with the contrast between the options 1—3 of our schema and option 4 we have reached a far point in tracing the logical sources of the difference between T and non-T. It is a stubborn difference because it is elusive; often as elusive to those who are sympathetic to the hermeneutic(s) of suspicion as to those opposed. It seems clear in any event that when T and non-T get to the point of polarization, the problem is not just a logical difference, but a difference of logics. The schema just described is one effort to say what those logics might be.

Finally, for the sake of discussion, one further hypothesis. We have seen that while the peculiar insistence of suspicion has a logical dimension, what absorbs its advocates is the ethical. We have also seen that for non-T there is, one way or another, a reciprocal relationship between the (truly) ethical and the (truly) religious. But it seems possible to go a step further. Very much in the spirit of non-T, the theologian J. B. Metz writes, "The shortest definition of religion: interruption."[6] With this Metz goes beyond saying that religious conviction may entail the interrupting of certain processes. He implies that the interruption itself is religious. Thus my final suggestion. Where the press toward a point of unity is viewed under the aspect of totalization, the very occurrence of interruption will be regarded as a "breaking open," a moment of grace—a virtual hierophany.

Notes

1 Paul Tillich, *Theology of Culture* (New York: Oxford University Press, 1964), 10–29.

2 Tillich, *op. cit.*, 25; emphasis added.

3 *Ibid.*, 26; emphasis added.

4 See Stephen Toulmin, *The Uses of Argument* (Cambridge: Cambridge University Press, 1958), 94–145.

5 The schema is drawn from my book, *Theology and Difference: The Wound of Reason* (Bloomington: Indiana University Press, 1993), 49–50.

6 Johann Baptist Metz, *Faith in History and Society: Toward a Practical Fundamental Theology* (New York: Seabury Press, 1980), 171.

4

The Pros and Cons of Theism
Whether They Constitute the Fundamental Issue
of the Philosophy of Religion

Stephen Crites

I have noticed, without taking any formal surveys, that there seems to be a confusing diversity of practice among self-described philosophers of religion, not all of it guild-related. Let us, for courtesy and convenience, speak of the philosophy of religion as a field, though it is more like a zoo, with each enclosure exhibiting yet another exotic species. The attractions of the dyad being what they are, it would be heartening to think that in the welter of different ways we write and teach and think in this, well, this field, a discerning taxonomist could descry two clear types into which all of us could for some purpose or other be sorted out, and could show how the two types correspond to two guilds: APA and AAR.

For purposes of these comments, I am prepared to suspend my scepticism about handy dyads and to succumb to their attractions. The two types placed on the agenda of this forum do seem to enjoy some tenuous and provocative hold on reality, and the difference is worth exploring. In this indulgent frame of mind, I might also suggest that the broad difference in the practice of this field in the two academic guilds is replicated on many campuses in departments of philosophy and departments of religious studies respectively. The fact that I myself have taught philosophy of religion in each of these departments in various institutions and at various times in my career gives me pause, but the experience does serve to confirm that there are characteristic differences in the way the field is contextualized in the two departments.

For instance, since the formation of the AAR in the mid-sixties the study of religion in a typical department has been cross-cultural. Its curriculum no longer resembles that of a Catholic or Protestant seminary. Its faculty includes specialists in Judaica, in Buddhism and Hinduism, in the History of Religions in the University of Chicago mold, and its students take specialized courses in these areas. Philosophers of religion in such departments are influenced by the wide-ranging studies and interests of their colleagues, and they confront different questions in their classrooms than they would from students who had only been exposed to dominant Western religions, questions that reflect the ritual practices, the social formations, the belief systems, the moral codes from religions around the world that their students have been studying in other courses. The kinds of philosophical inquiries they are prepared to discuss in class and in departmental colloquia had better be broad and deep enough to accommodate issues to which these studies have given rise, and not only to those that have arisen, say, from the beliefs and practices of Christian theism. This cross-cultural development in religious studies antedates by decades the more recent multi-cultural experiments across the entire curriculum, and reflects a near-consensus of long standing that it is the appropriate way of structuring the study of religion in the university. Philosophy departments, on the other hand, have their own reasons, some good and some perhaps bad, for resisting multi-culturalism. The good reasons have to do with the integrity and cultural independence of philosophical inquiry itself. Philosophers, like scientists, have not been quick to yield to the facile description of their discipline as a mere cultural product, like skirts and trousers, nor to the cultural relativism such descriptions presuppose. A result of this resistance, perhaps a contingent and not necessary result, is that practitioners of our field in most departments of philosophy have continued to privilege the quandaries of Western theism, which do seem culturally specific, as their given subject matter.

But faculty and students in departments of religious studies not only typically know more about the religions than their counterparts in the APA. They also know and care more about "religion": not merely about the intentional objects of religious belief and prayer and terror and sacrifice, which are already various, but also about social patterns and practices, ritual cultus, sacred spaces, gender relations, sacred texts in literate religions and sacred forests in non-literate; about burial practices, sacramental elements and fetishes, totems and taboos, myths of creation and nation founding and destruction, and, as the admen say, much, much more. To explore such subjects, the methods of religious studies departments are typically interdisciplinary. Philosophers or philosopher/phenomenologists typically find themselves cheek by jowl with sociologists, anthropologists, psychologists (alas), text critics, and historians of many different stripes. They not only meet regularly with this motley crowd, but find their own discipline contextualized and impinged upon by these others. It has often been said that religion is a subject matter rather than a discipline, but the multiple disciplines employed to study it have arguably been shaped by the study to form the makings of a new discipline compounded of its parent disciplines. In this ensemble or compound, philosophers of religion continue to press philosophical questions, including critical questions about the other disciplines, but they do so in a cognitive space they share with them as well.

To some extent this is true of all the "philosophy of…" subfields of philosophy, philosophy of science, philosophy of art, etc., that are practiced in a department of philosophy. At the same time, their inquiries are rooted in the "pure" philosophical disciplines of logic and dialectics, metaphysics, epistemology, ethics. Without that root they would have nothing to contribute to these interdisciplinary dialogues. Now that is also true of the philosopher of religion in a department of religious studies. But in a department of philosophy practitioners of this field typically find their work contextualized primarily by the great intra-mural conversation of philosophy itself, which has extended from Greek antiquity to the present. Here the status of the gods or the High God have been acceptable topics, but not generally the mere mortal practice of religion. Underlying every manifest topic of this long conversation, furthermore, has been the self-referential debate about the nature and correct method of philosophy itself.

One more excursion into academic sociology, perhaps still more tendentious than the above, and then we will mercifully turn to a little philosophy. Since Kant the great conversation of philosophy has tended to divide into two, with only occasional interchange between them, the one conducted in the English language, the other in the continental European languages, primarily in German and French. These two conversations of modern times have been irreconcilably divided over what we have called the self-referential debate: what is philosophy? Each has continued to agitate this question, but between the two this question has engendered irreconcilable conflict, regrettably to the present day. With noble exceptions the parties to these two conversations have been scarcely on speaking terms.

The bearing of this dismal breach within philosophy upon our present question appears to me to be this: Practitioners of our field in departments of religious studies today tend, with some exceptions, to be nourished by the continental schools, by Kant and Hegel, Marx and Kierkegaard and Nietzsche, Heidegger and Gadamer and Merleau-Ponty, and in some quarters even by the frivolous post-modernist French (*hélas!*). Why this should be so is a long story that we will cut short with the observation that the continental schools have had a broadly humanistic orientation, a tradition of cultural engagement, hermeneutic and criticism, well adapted to philosophical studies in the human practice of religion. Very technical, formal issues are certainly addressed in this tradition, but they bear fairly directly on existential concerns regarding conditions for the good life. Departments of philosophy in Britain and in this country, on the other hand, have been dominated, again with notable exceptions (probably more exceptions, in fact), by the recent Anglo-American schools that have been lumped under the label of "analytic philosophy." Philosophers of religion in these departments have largely debated the merits, the claim to meaning and truth, of the prevailing theism in English-speaking countries. Its philosophical apologists have constructed a rigorous new scholasticism employing the logical-empiricist instruments of the analytic school. Its philosophical critics have attacked the coherence of theistic beliefs employing the same instruments. At its best this debate is conducted with a clarity and rigor that it owes to the scientific model of analytic philosophy generally.

A curious shibboleth serves to identify the members of the two schools. Philosophers nourished by the continental school pronounce the name of the great father of this school, Kant, in the German manner: "Kahnt." Analytic philosophers, following the English custom of anglicizing foreign names and cities around the world, call him Can't, perhaps because they can't understand him, or can't abide him.

In his most well-known discussions of God's existence, Kant, remarkably, exhibited the abiding tendencies of each of the schools in turn. In the First *Kritik* he rejected the traditional arguments for God's existence on grounds of logical incoherence and empirical vacuity, the very terms on which the issue has generally been debated, positively and negatively, in the Anglo-American school. In the second *Kritik* he postulated God's existence as a necessary condition for a moral world order vindicating human freedom. In the continental school, and among its adherents in the provinces, the burning issue concerning the existence of God has continued to be whether it is a necessary ground of personal and/or political freedom or whether it implies the radical denial of such freedom. Here, it appears to me, we find the deepest intellectual ground for the observed breach between philosophers of religion typically affiliated with our two guilds.

Though the AAR crowd certainly addresses concepts of gods, goddesses, High Gods and sundry numinoi, both positively and negatively, it is generally a fact that it does not consider issues surrounding these concepts as such to be philosophically fundamental. There are many reasons for this fact, in detail, and wide disagreements about which reasons for it are the decisive ones. Without presuming to speak for the whole crowd, I will conclude these remarks simply by summarizing my own reasons.

So now at last to the question.

Whether the pros and cons of theism constitute the fundamental issue in the philosophy of religion?

Obj. 1. It seems that the pros and cons of theism constitute the fundamental issue in the philosophy of religion. For as the Philosopher says in the *Logik* (Lasson ed., vol. I, p. 63), "and God has the most undisputed right, that with him the Beginning [of philosophical science] should be made." Since God is the supreme fullness of Being, all consideration of the things that are must begin with God.

Obj. 2. Further, the cultural particularism of theistic belief is no ground for denying that its pros and cons may be the fundamental issue for philosophers in that tradition. As Wolterstorff points out, analytic philosophers who have moved beyond Kantian interpretation-universalism and metaphysical anti-realism may unabashedly address their philosophical debates to the particularism of traditional theism in the West.

Obj. 3. Further, given the power of God to bless and to damn, philosophers cannot suppose that they can deny with impunity that the pros and cons of theism occupy the position of fundamental issue in philosophy of religion.

Obj. 4. "Further, the existence of truth is self-evident. For whoever denies the existence of truth grants that truth does not exist: and, if truth does not exist, then the proposition *Truth does not exist* is true: and if there is anything true, there must be truth. But God is truth itself." Therefore the pros and cons of theism constitute the fundamental issue in the philosophy of religion.

Sed Contra, the Philosopher says in the Preface to the *Phaenomenologie des Geistes* (Hoffmeister ed., p. 54), "it may be useful to avoid the name *God* [in philosophical science], because this word is not at the same time immediately a concept, but rather the proper name, the fixed point of rest of the underlying subject; whereas, on the other hand, e.g. Being or the One, Particularity, the Subject, themselves also immediately signify concepts."

Responsio: As the Philosopher goes on to observe, the introduction of the word, "God," into philosophical discourse tends to divert it into mere edification. What for piety or edification may be supreme must in the logic of philosophical discourse always be subordinate to more conceptually manageable or more empirically available concepts. Philosophers who have undertaken to speak rigorously of God have inevitably done so by way of more determinate concepts and categories. For to speak of God at all, even for the sake of denying the divine existence, is to assume that by this word something of unutterable significance is intended, but for that very reason any literal and unmediated reference to God is conceptually vacuous. Traditionally philosophers have either claimed that God can be referred to conceptually only in negations, or through various stand-ins, such as Being, Prime Mover, Substance, Perfection itself, etc. In the latter case, although they intend to be speaking of the God of devout believers, they instead speak of prototypical Being, to be approached through general ontological categories, or of Prime Mover, through categories of motion or causality, or Perfection, through categories of value, or Eternity, through temporal categories, and the like. More recently, frankly naturalistic or anthropological terms have been used analogically, employing moral, aesthetic, scientific, conative, voluntaristic categories, or Austinian speech-act theory, but in all such analogies there is many a slip 'twixt the cup and the lip. More forthright are philosophers who have enjoined silence regarding that of which one cannot speak. This rule of silence does not prohibit the faithful from speaking *to* God, in prayer or hymn, but the grammatical turn to third person referential language *about* God always risks trivialization, if not outright blasphemy. Here the best recourse is metaphor, typology, and indirection.

If talk about God is otherwise always a bloodless abstraction, "theism" is an abstraction of the second order, a generic term situated in discourse by juxtaposition with "pantheism," "polytheism," "atheism," of use only in making distinctions within a categorization of great generality. For a philosophy of religion committed to the critical examination of issues arising out of the living practice of religion, "theism" is of very limited importance. The putative literalism of philosophical talk about theism is purchased at the price of religious and existential irrelevance.

Reply Obj. 1. The philosopher goes on to remark that this "undisputed right" would hold if its intuition implied more than pure being, which he holds to be the emptiest of all categories. But "let what is present in intuition or figurate conception be as rich as it may, the determination which *first* appears in knowing is simple, for only in what is simple is there nothing more than pure beginning....Consequently, whatever is intended to be expressed or implied beyond *being*, in the richer forms of representing the absolute or God, this is in the beginning only an empty word and only being."

Reply Obj. 2. There is nothing to prevent philosophers from talking about whatever interests them, however parochial it may be. Thus a hockey fan might well philosophize about hockey. But to do so the philosophical fan would have to approach his subject through considerations less parochial than hocky itself. Even post-Kantian philosophy must observe the criterion of universality, at least as a regulative principle, in its fundamental terms of discussion.

Reply Obj. 3. The gods of the philosophers not being the God of Abraham, Isaac, and Jacob, there is a great hiatus between the prophetic oracles of God and consideration of the pros and cons of theism. Thus a reticence concerning the latter may be less culpable than overmuch confident talk. For as the Prophet Thaddeus of Middle Haddam has been heard to declare, All theistic chatter is a stench in the nostrils of the Almighty. His companion at the cracker barrel, Lucius the Village Atheist, dismisses it as so much twaddle. Philosophical papers from our Jewish students omit the vowel from references to God, in reverence for the G-d's unutterable sacredness, even, comically enough, when they are denying G-d's existence.

Reply Obj. 4. "The existence of truth in general is self-evident, but the existence of a Primal Truth is not self-evident to us."

5
The Cultural Anthropology
of Philosophy and Religion
Philip L. Quinn

Philosophy of religion is a practice within the discipline of philosophy, and it is also a practice in religious studies. There are striking differences between the way in which it is practiced in philosophy's main professional association in the United States, the American Philosophical Association (APA), and the way in which it is practiced in the corresponding institution for religious studies, the American Academy of Religion (AAR). How are those differences best understood? This essay is devoted to reflection on that question. In it I explore the suggestion that, because the objects of study are social practices, description and explanation of the differences should be framed in cultural and historical terms.

The essay has four parts. The first sets the stage by describing what I am going to do as if it were a research project in cultural anthropology. The second and third are devoted to observations about aspects of the culture and history of philosophy and religious studies in the United States. The fourth part draws tentative conclusions from these observations. My argument is that the practices of philosophy of religion in philosophical institutions and in their counterparts in religious studies are, in some important respects, complementary. If I am right, more interaction between the practitioners of philosophy of religion in the two kinds of institution might well be mutually beneficial.

I. A Research Project in Cultural Anthropology
There is a society made up of people who think of themselves as the academics. A large and flourishing part of it inhabits the United States. It is a tribal society. Since members of one of its tribes typically live in villages called "departments of philosophy," I shall call this tribe "the philosophy tribe." Members of the philosophy tribe practice many crafts; one of them is philosophy of religion. Three times each year members of the philosophy tribe from all over the United States gather to perform rituals. These ritual gatherings are the annual meetings of the Eastern, Central and Pacific Divisions of the APA. At them practitioners of various philosophical crafts display the products of their crafts. So if one wants to see how the craft of

philosophy of religion is practiced by the philosophy tribe, one can look at the displays at the annual ritual gatherings of the APA.

I am a member of the philosophy tribe. I have spent almost all of my professional life living in one or another of its villages. I have participated many times in the ritual gatherings of the APA. Indeed, having been president of the Central Division of the APA, I suppose it is fair to say that I have been honored by my tribe by having been chosen to serve for a time as one of its ritual chiefs. I practice the craft of philosophy of religion. Hence I speak with the authority of a native informant about the folkways of the philosophy tribe in general and about its practice of the craft of philosophy of religion in particular.

The craft of philosophy of religion is also practiced by members of another tribe. Since its members often live in villages called "departments of religious studies," I shall call this tribe "the religious studies tribe." Once a year members of the religious studies tribe from villages all over the United States gather to perform rituals. This ritual gathering is the annual meeting of the AAR. At it practitioners of various crafts, including philosophy of religion, display their wares. If one wants to see how the craft of philosophy of religion is practiced by the religious studies tribe, one can look at the displays at the annual ritual gathering of the AAR.

I am not a member of the religious studies tribe, but I have more than a nodding acquaintance with its folkways. I lived for a while in one of its villages as a participant-observer, when I taught for a semester in Princeton's Department of Religion. I have also twice participated by invitation in the annual ritual gathering of the AAR. So I am in a position to speak with some authority about the practice of philosophy of religion in the religious studies tribe. But what I say stands subject to correction by its native informants.

It is worth mentioning that there are some villages in which members of these two tribes live together. Often they are called "departments of philosophy and religion." Such villages tend to be unstable. Frequently they split into separate philosophy villages and religious studies villages.

My observations of the displays of the craft of philosophy of religion at the ritual gatherings of the APA and the AAR give me the impression that there are large differences between the way philosophy of religion is practiced in the philosophy tribe and the way it is practiced in the religious studies tribe. To be sure, there are enough similarities to insure that it is not by sheer equivocation that the things being compared from the two tribes have the same name. Fortunately, both tribes are literate, and so one can confirm the impression of difference in the texts they produce. An interesting research project in cultural anthropology would be to describe and explain these differences. I am qualified to take part in this research because I can speak as a native informant about the practices of one of the tribes and as a participant-observer in the practices of the other. No doubt it will not be easy to secure funding to support this research. So I propose to begin doing it without grant support in what follows.

II. Tales of My Own Tribe

For the most part, leading philosophers of religion who practice their craft in philosophy departments work in the analytic style, have fairly traditional theistic beliefs, and devote their efforts to explicating and defending those beliefs. I speak of the analytic style because I do not want to suggest that there is much agreement on matters of doctrine among analytic philosophers. Analytic philosophers have been influenced by a tradition that in this century goes back to Moore and Russell; they prize such intellectual virtues as expository clarity and argumentative rigor; and they make use of techniques of philosophical analysis in their work. There are, of course, leading philosophers of religion who are not analytic philosophers; Stephen Evans and Merold Westphal are examples. The traditional theistic beliefs of which I speak are in most cases parts of distinctively Christian world-views. There are also leading philosophers of religion who are not Christians; Richard Gale, William Rowe and George Schlesinger are examples. When the exceptions have been noted, however, there remains a group that includes Marilyn Adams, Robert Adams, William Alston, William Hasker, Peter van Inwagen, Norman Kretzmann, George Mavrodes, Alvin Plantinga, James Ross, Eleonore Stump, William Wainwright, Edward Wierenga, Nicholas Wolterstorff and Linda Zagzebski, among others.[1] These Christian philosophers are engaged in the traditional enterprise characterized as faith seeking understanding. Some of them would prefer describing what they do as philosophical theology to describing it as philosophy of religion. What accounts for the prominence of this group in the practice of philosophy of religion associated with the APA? I think this question is best answered by means of an historical narrative.

Approximately four decades ago American philosophy was in the grip of a passion to become scientific or at least to become a metascientific discipline. This passion was most forcefully expressed first in logical positivism and then later in logical empiricism. A verificationist account of meaning was deployed to demarcate between meaningful and meaningless claims. It was hoped that criteria of cognitive significance could be formulated according to which all scientific claims would turn out to be meaningful and most of the claims of traditional theism would not. Philosophers of religion were preoccupied with religious language. Some argued that religious claims are cognitively significant because they can be verified eschatologically after death. Others proposed noncognitivist accounts of the meaning of religious claims. Yet others argued that verificationist theories of meaning should be rejected. But this debate about religious language was not of much interest to most American philosophers. During my years as a graduate student, no graduate courses or seminars in philosophy of religion were offered at the university where I studied. Philosophy of religion was widely regarded as an intellectual backwater. I suppose this influential attitude helps to explain why many of the older members of the group now committed to doing Christian philosophical theology were not trained in philosophy of religion as graduate students. The research agendas of other areas of philosophy were then more exciting than that of philosophy of religion. And indeed quite a few of these philosophers began their careers by making strong contributions to research in such areas as history of philosophy, metaphysics, epistemology, philosophy of language and philosophy of science.

But American culture changed. Science bore some bitter fruit and lost some of its prestige. The worship of science came to look like nothing more than a new form of idolatry. The influence of logical positivism and logical empiricism waned in philosophy. It became possible to reopen questions in philosophical theology that had been neglected when debates about religious language dominated philosophy of religion and to draw on resources from other areas of philosophy in addressing them. Modern modal logic was employed in formulating more precise versions of the ontological argument for the existence of God and of the free will defense against the logical problem of evil. Work on essences in metaphysics was applied in discussions of divine attributes such as omniscience and omnipotence. And epistemological work on externalism and internalism was used to clarify issues concerning the rationality, justification or warrant of traditional theistic beliefs. As I see it, the result of these activities has been to show that least some parts of theistic world-views are at least as respectable, philosophically speaking, as the main rival world-views such as naturalism that are available to us in present circumstances of philosophical and religious pluralism. And it is not surprising that, recently, philosophers who are Christian theists have been trying to extend this result to include such distinctively Christian doctrines as the Trinity, the Incarnation and the Atonement.

Nor is it surprising that philosophers who are theists should have taken the lead in bringing about this small renaissance of philosophical theology. Philosophers who are indifferent to religion can find plenty of other exciting topics to investigate in other areas of the discipline. A complacent atheism is so deeply ensconced in the culture of American academics that even passionate atheists, with only a few exceptions, find it easier to dismiss theism as an outdated superstition than to argue against it. In such a culture it is only to be expected that theists will be the philosophers who care most about the philosophical credentials of theism and will be motivated to defend it if the philosophical resources available to them make such a defense look like a promising project. And perhaps there is a relatively straightforward demographic explanation of the large percentage of Christians among such theistic philosophers.

The revival of philosophical theology within analytic philosophy has been accompanied by some interesting developments in the ways in which analytic philosophers of religion respond to the history of philosophy. Analytic philosophers tend to view their predecessors as interlocutors rather than as museum pieces; they will tell one with a tone of pride that they are not mere historians of ideas. They find conversation partners among the medievals and modern philosophers before Kant. After all, such philosophers were, for the most part, theists of a traditional sort themselves; they valued clarity and rigor; and they employed many of the techniques of philosophical analysis in their work. Kant is seen as a transitional figure, perhaps admired for the nobility of his attempt to include a good deal of the content of traditional Christian theology within the limits of reason alone but regarded as dangerous because of his influence on subsequent developments in European philosophy and theology, particularly those in Germany. But analytic philosophical theology has been unable to appropriate the work of most continental European philosophers and theologians of the nineteenth and twentieth centuries or even to come to grips with it in a serious way, Kierkegaard being the exception that proves the rule but only a partial exception. Since such work is not analytic in style, this is not surprising. What is more, the philosophical tradition that proceeds from Hegel through Feuerbach and Marx to Nietzsche and the theological tradition that runs from Schleiermacher to Ritschl, as well as the twentieth century continuations of such traditions, depart, more or less radically, from the theistic doctrines most analytic philosophical theologians are trying to defend. As a result, these traditions are almost entirely ignored in analytic philosophical theology, which produces a kind of scholarship whose range of historical reference is restricted to philosophy before Kant and books and journal articles in analytic philosophy from the past two or three decades. Those who see positive developments in the traditions thus ignored or who think they define the context for productive philosophical thought about religion at the present time are therefore apt to view analytic philosophy of religion as both insensitive to history and terminally nostalgic.

III. Observations of the Others

I find it helpful to think about religious studies in terms of an analogy with the emerging interdisciplinary field of science studies. In science studies, scientific theory and practice are the objects of study. Scientific theory and practice are fairly well defined parts of culture, and they can be studied using the methods and tools of various disciplines that investigate cultural phenomena. Contributions to science studies are made by philosophers of science, historians of science, sociologists of science, psychologists of science and even a few anthropologists. A practitioner of a science can also study it, but one can study a science without also being a practitioner of it. And one can study a science without sharing the scientific beliefs of its practitioners. The study of a science is done from a point of view external to the science being studied. Adopting such an external point of view is one of the ways in which objectivity is secured in science studies.

In religious studies, religious theory and practice are the objects of study. Religious theory and practice are fairly well defined parts of culture, and they can be investigated with the tools and techniques of various disciplines that study cultural phenomena. Contributions to religious studies are made by philosophers of religion, historians of religions, sociologists of religion, psychologists of religion and quite a few anthropologists. A practitioner of a religion can also study it, but one need not be a practitioner of a religion in order to study it. And one can study a religion without sharing the religious beliefs of its practitioners. The study of a religion is done from a point of view external to the religion being studied. Adopting such an external point of view is one of the ways in which objectivity is secured in religious studies.

In the American context, it is politically useful—and I am sure it is no accident—that religious studies is constituted in roughly the way described above. Practitioners of religious studies can legitimately claim that they are not involved in any way in religious proselytizing because they work outside all theological circles. They can then argue successfully that religious studies can be taught in tax-supported schools without breaching the constitutional wall of separation between church and state. I conjecture that the need to be sensitive to the constitutional issue puts a certain amount of pressure on philosophers of religion who work in religious studies to keep their own religious views out of their teaching and research. By doing so they support their discipline's claim to objectivity.

The external point of view that approaches the status of being the official stance of religious studies toward religions enables its practitioners to exclude their personal religious beliefs from their professional work. The articulation and defense of one's personal religious beliefs is generally thought not to be included in one's job description in religious studies. I actually have no idea whether most of the leading philosophers of religion in religious studies are traditional theists. I suspect not. But even if they were, it would not be easy to discern it in the sort of work they typically present at meetings of the AAR. By design, religious studies is constituted in such a way that there is no easy inference from one's scholarly work to one's personal religious commitments or lack thereof. Indeed, on one or two occasions I have gotten the impression that, in religious studies circles, it is considered to be in bad taste to introduce one's personal religious views into serious academic conversation. Adopting a phrase from Richard Rorty, one might say, with only a slight air of paradox, that in religious studies religion is a conversation-stopper.[2]

The philosophers of religion who inhabit departments of religious studies have as their immediate colleagues and primary conversation partners historians, sociologists and anthropologists rather than metaphysicians, epistemologists and logicians. No doubt this helps to explain why they take social scientific explanations of religious beliefs with a seriousness that the philosophers of religion in departments of philosophy do not accord them. However, the social sciences in their modern form did not exist before Kant, although there are, of course, plenty of observations that would be grist for a social scientist's mill in the works of writers such as Montaigne. The classics of sociology of religion are, after all, works by Durkheim and Weber. Such works have their philosophical roots in, and are best understood in the context of, a tradition of nineteenth century European philosophy that goes back from Marx through Feuerbach to Hegel. So it is no surprise that philosophers of religion in religious studies have an interest in this tradition in continental philosophy; nor is it surprising that they are also interested in its continuation and further development in the twentieth century. Such philosophers are apt to think that philosophy before Kant was very naive about the extent to which religious realities are socially constructed cultural products, and so they are likely to suspect that philosophy before Kant, apart from a few exceptional cases such as Vico, is almost entirely of only anti-quarian interest.

If I am right, the differences between the practices of the philosophers of religion associated with the APA and the practices of the philosophers of religion associated with the AAR are to be explained, at least in part, by differences in the cultural environments that surround the two groups in virtue of their different social locations in the academy. I have indicated, albeit in a sketchy way, some of the cultural factors I regard as having explanatory promise. Undoubtedly my sketch would need to be filled out in order to be made into a convincing realistic portrait. And it would be desirable for the filling out to be done and the necessary corrections made by a real cultural anthropologist, who could provide more than the sort of impoverished arm-chair anthropology to which I am restricted by limits on my competence. Still, I hope that I have provided some hypotheses that are worth discussing and could be subjected to empirical tests should anyone consider such an enterprise worthwhile. But how are we to respond to the situation I have described and tried to explain? In concluding, I address this question by making some explicitly evaluative remarks.

IV. Conclusions

When I reflect on the differences between philosophy of religion in the philosophy tribe and philosophy of religion in the religious studies tribe, I see a picture of practices that tend to have complementary strengths and weaknesses. Four of them are especially salient.

First, philosophers of religion in the philosophy tribe tend to focus their attention exclusively on questions of the consistency, rationality or truth of theological doctrines, while philosophers of religion in the religious studies tribe tend to ignore doctrinal questions in order to focus on other aspects of religion such as ritual and myth. Both tendencies are obstacles to achieving a comprehensive philosophical understanding of religion. There are many interesting philosophical questions about the affective and social dimensions of religious life that are not related to issues of doctrinal orthodoxy. But, though orthodoxy is not the whole of any religion, it is an important part of many religions, and the philosophical questions it raises should not be ignored.

Second, philosophers of religion in the religious studies tribe tend to be rather quick to adopt ideas from recent continental European philosophy and to accept social scientific explanations of religious phenomena, while philosophers of religion in the philosophy tribe tend to ignore recent continental European philosophy and to be hostile to social scientific explanations of religious phenomena. Again both tendencies get in the way of achieving a balanced philosophical perspective on religion. No doubt recent French philosophy, for example, contains valuable ideas, but a good deal of it seems to be little more than a parade of the latest fashions in Parisian intellectual circles. And, though social scientific explanations of religious phenomena are sometimes sources of insight, often they are speculations poorly supported by empirical evidence. Surely what all good philosophers of religion need is a receptivity to ideas that come from those sources coupled with a willingness to subject them to the test of criticism.

Third, philosophers of religion in the philosophy tribe tend to act as if they believe that, leaving aside Kierkegaard and perhaps Newman, nothing of philosophical interest was said about religion between Kant and Plantinga, while philosophers of religion in the religious studies tribe tend to act as if they believe that, leaving aside Hume, nothing that can contribute to the contemporary philosophical understanding of religion was said before Kant and that medieval and early modern philosophical thought on religious topics is now of interest only to historians of ideas. Both tendencies underestimate the resources available to philosophers of religion in the whole of the history of Western philosophy.

Fourth, philosophers of religion in the religious studies tribe tend to stress the idea that religion is a socially constructed cultural product to an extent that makes it difficult, if not impossible, to steer clear of various pernicious varieties of relativism, while philosophers of religion in the philosophy tribe tend to ignore issues of social construction and cultural context altogether, treating religious beliefs or propositions as timeless and ahistorical Platonic entities. Once again both tendencies are likely to block the road of inquiry. No doubt religious belief systems are social constructs and should be regarded, for the most part, as fallible and open to further development and revision. But scientific belief systems too are social constructs, and this does not prevent scientists from sometimes discovering nonrelativistic truths and acquiring genuine knowledge of them. So it is possible to acknowledge that religious belief systems are social constructs without denying that there is religious knowledge of nonrelativistic truths.

In order to make the four contrasts I have drawn between the practices of the philosophers of religion in the two tribes stand out in sharp relief, I have, I realize, been painting with a broad brush, neglecting nuances and subtle qualifications. But if the picture I have painted has even the accuracy of a good caricature, the moral to be drawn from it is obvious. The philosophers of religion from the two tribes should get better acquainted. The two groups have much to learn from one another; each would bring to the encounter strengths that could serve as correctives to the other's weaknesses.

Notes

[1] Intellectual and religious autobiographies of many of these people are to be found in Kelly James Clark (ed.), *Philosophers Who Believe* (Downers Grove, IL: Inter Varsity Press, 1993) and Thomas V. Morris (ed.), *God and the Philosophers* (New York: Oxford University Press, 1994).

[2] Richard Rorty, "Religion as Conversation-Stopper," *Common Knowledge* 3,1 (1994). Commenting on Stephen Carter's *The Culture of Disbelief,* Rorty argues that religion is a conversation-stopper in political discussion.

6

On Taking God Seriously
Philosophy of Religion in the APA and AAR

C. Stephen Evans

My professional identity and training are centered in the discipline of philosophy. As an undergraduate I managed to satisfy most of the religion requirements at my school by taking examinations; during my graduate studies at Yale I never even considered taking courses in theology or at the divinity school, even though the philosophy department would have allowed this and I can see in retrospect that I would have profited greatly from doing so. I have never taught in a department of theology or religious studies, and in the early stages of my career I rarely read professional journals that were not philosophical in character.

All of the above helps explain why it is that when I was invited to participate at an AAR/SBL annual meeting in the early eighties, I am not sure I was even aware of the existence of those professional organizations, though of course I thought that teachers of religion had some kind of professional association. Nevertheless, I have now been a member of the AAR for more than ten years and have attended most of the annual meetings during that time, chiefly because of the on-going discussions of Kierkegaard that occurred there.

I therefore have some acquaintance with both sides of the AAR-APA split in the philosophy of religion. However, the reader should be forewarned that I am not a neutral party in disputes between the two groups. I have often felt a strong sense of alienation at AAR annual meetings, a consciousness of being "different" if not "other". I have sometimes felt like a "stranger in a strange land," and at other times like a partisan who is operating in enemy-controlled territory.

The above is offered not only as a warning but also as anecdotal evidence that the perceived differences between philosophy of religion in the AAR and APA are not completely illusory. The differences are of course not absolute, and there are many exceptions to generalizations about the seriousness with which theism is taken or not taken, both in the APA and AAR. There are plenty of traditional theists at AAR meetings and plenty of APA philosophers who are uninterested in questions about the reality of a personal God.

Nevertheless, there are differences in what we might call the cultures of the AAR and APA. Even though at an APA meeting, the official program is controlled by one centralized committee (unlike the AAR, which to me resembles a medieval kingdom replete with fiefdoms of various ranks), and even though philosophy of religion is clearly somewhat marginal in the prestige pecking-order of the APA, it is often the case that there are more papers at an APA meeting that take seriously questions about traditional religious faith than there are at an AAR meeting. And this holds true despite the fact that at the AAR almost the entire program is devoted to religion in some form or other, and despite the fact that the AAR annual meeting as a whole is several times larger than even the largest APA meeting, which does not have one large annual convention but instead has three annual divisional meetings. I shall try to reflect these differences in culture by speaking of two mythical creatures, the APA philosopher of religion and the AAR philosopher of religion, while recognizing of course that the two types are to some degree caricatures.

I was not present at the session of the AAR where the initial four papers on this subject were presented, but I have had the pleasure of reading those papers. My own reflections on the presumed differences between philosophy of religion in the APA and AAR are partly shaped by my reactions to the thinking of others. In fact, much of what I wish to say on the topic has been said already by Wolterstorff and Westphal.

With Westphal I concur that philosophy departments have in general been more open to thinking about traditional religious questions than have departments of religious studies, mostly for sociological reasons that relate to the need of religious studies departments to justify their existence in an academy that frowns on religious commitments. Philosophers are thought to be eccentrics who tolerate all kinds of weird ideas, so it is not too surprising to find some religious people among their tribe, and others interested in debates about religious questions. I am, however, skeptical about Westphal's suggestion that these philosophical debates are remote enough from actual religious experience to be "safe." They at least do not appear to be so to many philosophers, who react with great hostility to affirmations of religious belief. A well-known philosopher brought in to lead a seminar on the mind-body problem at a church-related college, when asked what bearing belief in God might have on the problem, became both incredulous and angry, dismissing the question with a half-humorous but disturbing quip: "When I hear talk about God, I reach for my gun."

I also agree with Westphal's observation that the split between the APA and AAR has at least some correlation with the split between "analytic" and "continental" philosophy. However, as he himself points out, this observation does not take us very far, since the philosophical divide he points to is more likely a symptom than a cause of the problem, and in any case I agree with Westphal's claim that there is no reason why theistic philosophers should not find plenty of useful work in the continental tradition. There is no good reason why philosophers interested in Kant, Kierkegaard, Hegel, Nietzsche, Heidegger, Gadamer, and Derrida should not be theists and interested in questions dealing with theism; at least I hope not since I consider myself one of that party. So after noting that AAR philosophers tend towards the "continental" style, we are still lacking an explanation of why they tend to take theism less seriously than their colleagues in the APA.

Nicholas Wolterstorff suggests that the difference is linked to the clash between two rival successors to classical foundationalism: Kantian interpretation-universalism that is linked to metaphysical anti-realism as opposed to unabashedly ungrounded particularism. This idea ties in with Westphal's suggestion, since interpretation-universalism is less common in "analytic" philosophy; I would describe it as a well-known and not uncommonly but by no means universally accepted view in analytic circles. This hypothesis of Wolterstorff's takes us more deeply into the heart of the matter, and it is also one with which I concur. But once more chicken and egg problems emerge: Do philosophers of religion in the AAR tend to take theism less seriously because they are anti-realists? Or could at least part of the story about why they tend to be anti-realists be that they do not take theism seriously?

I am inclined to think that the split is best understood if we closely examine the paper presented by Stephen Crites. Crites goes beyond merely trying to understand the differences, and as the title of his paper suggests,[1] to some degree attempts to answer the normative question as to which approach to the philosophy of religion is more promising. In doing so he expresses a number of attitudes and convictions about traditional theism that I take to be widespread among his colleagues in the AAR. What I wish to do is continue the conversation he has begun by critically examining some of those beliefs and attitudes. In doing so I will perhaps be contributing some understanding of the differences between at least some philosophers in the AAR and many in the APA, though I realize I may not be a very typical representative of either group. But I hope to explain why many APA philosophers are unconvinced by the reasons some AAR philosophers would give for taking theism less seriously, and to some degree argue that the APA philosophers are justified in their skepticism about their colleague's skepticism.

Some of the ideas I will discuss are explicitly suggested or endorsed by Crites. Others are only implicitly suggested by things he says, and he perhaps would not wish to endorse them. Whether Crites would do so or not is less important to me than whether the ideas are held, consciously or unconsciously, by significant numbers of AAR guild-members. I will therefore proceed, in the spirit of Kierkegaard, to consider three theses "possibly or actually attributable to Crites."

Thesis (1): *"Theism" is an abstraction dealing with second-order questions that are not closely connected to the living practices of religion.* Crites says, for example, that theism is "a generic term situated in discourse by juxtaposition with 'pantheism,' 'polytheism,' 'atheism,' of use only in making distinctions within a categorization of great generality."

Crites is undoubtedly right in maintaining that the term "theism" is an abstract term. Roughly, I take it that "theism" is a way of designating those religious beliefs that Christians, Jews, and Muslims, along with a not-insignificant number of Hindus and a sprinkling of people from other faiths and some who are not adherents of any particular religion at all, hold in common. It is indeed second-order discourse in the sense that it is rarely used by religious believers in the course of religious worship and practice, but only by those who are thinking *about* those religious beliefs and activities. This observation, however, has little bearing on the question of the utility of thinking about theism, for the philosophy of religion is necessarily an abstract discipline relative to concrete religious life. It is not itself worship and prayer, though it can be carried on in a worshipful and prayerful manner, but second-order thinking about such activities as worshipping and praying. It is indeed second-order discourse, but what else can philosophy of religion be? Perhaps the perceived problem is not merely that theism concerns second-order discourse and reflection, but that it is discourse that is remote from actual religious concerns and therefore not very helpful for reflection on those concerns. All I can say to this is that it seems to me to be evidently false. Theism is simply a way of talking about a significant number of the important beliefs of ordinary religious people, beliefs that inform the lives and religious practices of these people.[2] To ask whether theism is true is simply to ask whether or not there really is a God, a powerful personal being, genuinely worthy of worship, who created the world and human persons and holds them responsible and accountable for the conduct of their lives. Many ordinary believers have an intense interest in the question of the truth or falsity of their beliefs about God. They are deeply concerned about whether God is real, and whether or not he has dealings with human beings, answers prayers, and so on. This suggestion of Crites seems to me indefensible, but perhaps it may be defended by some theory about how language about God functions. I pass therefore to possible thesis number two.

Thesis (2): *Theism is a dubious set of doctrines because it requires us to talk about God in ways that exceed the limits of meaningful human language.* Crites bluntly tells us that "any literal and unmediated reference to God is conceptually vacuous." Crites makes the interesting suggestion later in his paper that although it may be legitimate to speak *to* God "in prayer or hymn," third-person language about God is problematic: "the grammatical turn to third person referential language *about* God always risks trivialization, if not outright blasphemy. Here the best recourse is metaphor, typology, and indirection." Since theism as a set of beliefs seems inescapably referential in this third-person manner, we have here a claim that theism should not be at the center of philosophical discussion because theism is itself philosophically dubious.

This is itself of course a philosophical claim, and a very interesting one at that, just the kind of thing APA philosophers love to sink their teeth into. Just to hint at some of the discussion that should ensue at this point, why should Crites think that *second* person language is innocent if referentiality is the issue? Must I not be able to refer to God in order to address him? And why should I assume that if talk about (or to) God is mediated it must therefore fail to be literal? Is it perhaps not also true that names that refer to human persons necessarily "trivialize" in the sense that they fail to capture the richness and complexity of an actual person, yet we do not for that reason think that meaningful true statements about human persons cannot be made, however much those statements leave out? To speak confessionally for a moment, what I find frustrating about AAR meetings is that the kinds of claims Crites here makes are so often *assumed*, and so infrequently discussed and debated.

The issues are hardly foreign to APA philosophers. For as Crites surely knows, a tremendous amount of the twentieth century analytic discussion of philosophy of religion has consisted of intricate debates about the nature of religious language. The challenge of logical empiricism, and the later more nuanced philosophies of language inspired by the later Wittgenstein, unleashed a complicated discussion of the ways in which God-talk functions, including a nuanced debate about the possibility of referential use. If this discussion has diminished in the last 15 years or so, my judgment is that this is because the majority of participants in the discussion concluded that those who would deny the possibility of reference for religious language held overly-restrictive and artificial theories of language, theories that not only failed to do justice to religious language but to ethical, political, and scientific discourse as well.

Of course, recalling Wolterstorff's discussion of interpretation-universalism and its anti-realistic corollary, one might think the problem lies with reference per se, and not with reference to God. But once more we have an underlying philosophical disagreement that deserves debate, not a to-be-taken-for-granted assumption about language that justifies ignoring traditional religious questions. And however that debate about language turns out, my own hunch is that it will have to do justice to the common sense way we understand discourse that refers to persons and objects in the world, a way that allows us to make sense of the fact that claims about persons and objects in the world can be true or false independently of our opinions. I think it highly likely that such an account will allow the religious believer to make similar claims about God.

That of course raises another philosophical issue, one that is touched on by Walter Lowe who wonders whether it is religiously and philosophically adequate to think of God as a personal being because he worries about whether one should think of God as a being at all. Does thinking of God in this way amount to what Lowe calls "the dubious practice of regarding God as a being among other beings?" But once more the interesting philosophical questions here are assumed rather than forthrightly confronted. The term "being" here seems to be confused with "creature." Why should we assume that a being must be finite and limited? Why can't there be an infinite being? I have always found attempts to think of God in ways that avoid thinking of him as a being as ultimately lacking in content, and I am tempted to echo Alvin Plantinga, who once replied, when asked whether God was a being, "Of course, what else is there to be?"

Perhaps, however, philosophical worries about the status of religious language are relatively superficial worries, and the real reasons for distrust of theism lie deeper. The last thesis gets closer to heart of the matter, in my judgment.

Thesis (3): *There are more important things for philosophers of religion to do than discuss the status of theism, which is a parochial and culturally relative set of beliefs*. There is a subtle but undeniable tone of condescension in this thesis, which is linked to a quasi-sociological explanation of the shortcomings of philosophy departments. Philosophers are somewhat parochial because of their situation. APA philosophers undoubtedly have their own worthwhile intellectual tradition to nourish them, but in comparison with their brothers and sisters in religious studies departments, they are thought to lack an expansive intellectual environment in which to do their work. "Faculty and students in departments of religious studies not only typically know more about the religions than their counterparts in the APA. They also know and care more about 'religion.'" By this claim I take it that Crites means that APA philosophers pay too little attention to religions other than Christianity, and that they pay too little attention to dimensions of religion other than intellectual beliefs. Philosophers in religious studies departments, by contrast, are forced by virtue of the interdisciplinary nature of the field into paying more attention to those areas.

I am tempted to respond by challenging Crites' premises here, citing the work of APA philosophers such as Lad Sessions, Merold Westphal, and Keith Yandell that manifestly do take seriously the claims made by the world religions. But on second thought I am inclined to concede, and not just for the sake of argument, that APA philosophers such as myself ought to know more about other religions and ought to give more attention to the non-cognitive dimensions of religious life. I think I am not alone in thinking this, and I see increasing attention to both areas of concern. The interesting question here is whether if APA philosophers did fully measure up to Crites' standards on these points, they would then concur with his judgment that their current concerns constitute a "privileging" of the "culturally specific" quandaries of western theism.

In one sense any intellectual concerns that anyone has must be "culturally specific." There can be no human intellectual inquiry that has no cultural and historical context. So I take it that the real force of Crites' remark here is given by his later comment that "there is nothing to prevent philosophers from talking about whatever interests them, however parochial it may be." Perhaps the suggestion is that in worrying about such questions as whether a personal God exists, APA philosophers are simply assuming that the beliefs bound up in their inherited cultural tradition are serious candidates for truth, while ignoring serious candidates from other cultural traditions.

I suppose Crites must be at least partially correct here. Philosophers are human beings and they are hardly immune from the failings and foibles common to the human race. Human beings are prone to take some intellec-

tual options to be, in the language of William James, "live options," and
James is surely right in saying that it is not purely rational considerations
that determine this. It is the widespread recognition of this fact that has led
to the collapse of classical foundationalist epistemology, and that ought in
my judgment to lead to the collapse of the liberal vision of the academic life
as devoted solely to the impartial dictates of Reason.

But the melancholy but also reassuring truth that philosophers are all-
too-human by no means settles the issue about the fundamental importance
of theism. Suppose there is indeed a personal God who created human beings. Suppose that our highest destiny as human beings involves knowing
and properly relating to this God. Suppose that eternal life with God is a real
possibility for humans. If these suppositions are truths, then how could it be
unimportant for human beings not to know such truths? If millions of humans over many centuries, in different religions and different cultures, believe them to be true or wonder whether they might be true, how could it be
parochial for philosophers of religion to reflect on such possibilities?

Just to lend some perspective, suppose that a new and terrible plague
emerged that threatened to wipe out huge numbers of lives in North and
South America, Europe, Africa, the Middle East and significant parts of
Asia? The thought that worry about such a plague would be "parochial" is
either comical or monstrous. But of course the geographical regions I have
described simply are the regions where theistic beliefs predominate, and
many theists would hold that not just temporal welfare, but the eternal destiny of all human beings are linked to questions about religious truth. And
many atheists would agree about the importance of the questions, which is
why APA discussions of theism have always included a vigorous contingent
of people who hold no religious beliefs. Believers and unbelievers can agree
about the importance of the questions, and also about the value of intellectual honesty in facing them. For there are numerous believing philosophers
who are inclined to agree with their atheistic colleagues that *if* our central
religious beliefs are false, it is important to face this fact squarely, and not
obscure the consequences with confusing talk about symbols or the value of
religious practices.

This leads me to my own suspicion about the deepest source of the difference between APA and AAR philosophy of religion. If I believe in a God
who created me and intended me for eternal life with him, how can I not regard this truth as important? If I don't believe in such a God but think his
existence is a real possibility, I will make the same judgment about the importance of the questions. If I don't believe in such a God and believe that

recognition of the falsity of such belief will be of great value to humans, I will make a similar judgment as to the importance of the issues. For whom, then, are the questions not important? I think they will be people who meet two conditions: they do not consider the truth of theism to be a live option, but they also do not consider it important to establish its falsity.

A non-theistic Hindu believer might, for example, concede that the claims of theism would be significant if they were true, but simply not think that truth to be a serious possibility. At the same time, such a person might have no inclination to argue for the falsity of theism, since he or she might think that theistic beliefs have practical value for those who hold them and perhaps even for society generally. Similar remarks could be made about many Buddhists. Some non-religious secular thinkers might be similarly inclined to regard the truth of theism to be too far-fetched to be worth considering, but unlike their evangelically atheistic co-believers, judge that the practical benefits of theistic beliefs for those who hold them outweigh the value of any campaign to extirpate them.

Their attitude might be similar to my attitude towards someone prophesying the end of the world next week. I am willing to concede that the claims of the prophet would be hugely significant if true but I am inclined to regard the likelihood of their truth as so small as not to merit any reflection on my part. But I don't think it worth my while to engage in any efforts to enlighten the poor soul, either, unless he threatens me or mine in some way. Of course if the prophet is a true prophet, then so much the worse for me, but that is a risk I am willing to take.

Note here that it is theoretically possible for me to take the attitude that I simply would not care about the truth of the prophecy even if it were true. However, unless I care nothing about the world and my life in it, such an attitude would be irrational. In a similar fashion, we can imagine many who might say that they are uninterested in theism, even if it is true. In my judgment, however, such an attitude, however prevalent it may be among secular intellectuals, is irrational except on the part of people who have no concern for their world and their destiny in it. For theism includes as an essential component claims about who human beings are in their relation to God, and an indifference to such claims *even if they are true* amounts to indifference to one's own true self.

A final category of people for whom theism is not a "live option" might be people for whom the questions are simply not well-formed. They cannot accept theism, but do not think it important to deny it, either, since the denial of a claim might be read as implying that the claim makes sense. If we remember that this is exactly the posture of logical positivism, we will recognize that more than this is necessary. Once more we need not only a sense that theistic belief is not a live option, but a corresponding sense that it is not important to make this clear to people. But this condition can of course be met. Just as was the case for the Hindu, Buddhist, or secular mind above, we can imagine someone who thinks that theistic beliefs, however logically ill-formed, have some pragmatic value, at least for the *hoi polloi*, such that the masses are better off unenlightened.

My own speculative guess is that among APA philosophers there is a relatively greater percentage of people who either (1) believe in theism; (2) would like to believe in theism or at least wonder about its truth in a concerned fashion; or (3) think that theism is false and also think that it would be a good thing if this falsity were more widely recognized. Conversely, among AAR philosophers of religions there is a greater percentage of people for whom theism is not a live option, for one reason or another, but who do not think it terribly important to make this generally known.

If I am even partly right about this, some interesting questions then emerge. Why is it the case that there are these different proportions in each field? Is it that people who tend towards one view gravitate towards one field? Or is it the case that socialization experiences as an undergraduate and in graduate school tend to produce one kind of mind-set? If the former is the case, why is it that more believers gravitate towards philosophy? Could it be that there is greater tolerance and openness to traditional religious faith in secular philosophy departments than in religious studies departments? If it is rather the case that people are changed by their academic experiences, once more questions are raised as to why this should be so. Is it merely a cultural accident? Are philosophers in one discipline simply doing better philosophy?

There is no non-tendentious way of answering such questions. One might think, for example, as Crites seems to, that philosophers who spent more time with Hindus or Buddhists would worry less about theism. But perhaps that is not the case. Perhaps more exposure to Hinduism and Buddhism would simply solidify the conclusion many theists, including some Hindu theists, have reached that non-theistic religious convictions are either unintelligible or vastly less plausible than theistic convictions.

Crites seems to wonder whether or not APA philosophers who were exposed to more psychologists of religion, sociologists of religion, and scholars of world religions, would change their interests somewhat. It is a fair question. But without doubting that such exposure would be beneficial, it is not obvious that the changes would include coming to believe that theistic beliefs are less than fundamentally important.

I wonder whether or not some AAR philosophers of religion who had more exposure to rigorous analytic philosophy would be quite so confident that traditional theistic beliefs were either false or unintelligible. Are there really good arguments to show that God cannot be understood as a being, or that human beings cannot meaningfully refer to God? Many of the philosophical discussions I have heard at the AAR seem to me to assume that Kant, Hume, Marx, Nietzsche, and Feuerbach have established more than they have.

My believing friends in the APA have read these philosophers too. We teach courses about such people, and we think we have read them carefully. Many of us have learned a lot from them, and we are in agreement that they have much to teach theists.[3] But we don't agree that they have shown that the truth of theism is unimportant.

Of course in a sense it isn't the *theory* that is important, but the living religious beliefs that contain theism as an element. And of course the religious importance of those beliefs has to be seen in the impact they make on the lives of the believers. Here I take some comfort from the interesting fact that Kierkegaard seems to be a major concern among analytic philosophers. A former editor of *Faith and Philosophy* informed me that he received more papers dealing with Kierkegaard than any other philosopher. This anecdotal evidence seems consistent with Walter Lowe's research. Among analytic, APA philosophers who publish in *Faith and Philosophy, Religious Studies,* and *International Journal for Philosophy of Religion*, Kierkegaard is by far and away the theologian who has been given the most attention. I think this suggests that such philosophy is neither remote from the real concerns of human existence nor impervious to "continental" thinkers.

As Kierkegaard reminds us, it will not do simply to say that one is interested in practical existential questions rather than the "abstract" concerns of theism. For no one was more passionately concerned with the questions of human existence than Kierkegaard, yet no one was more certain than he that they had to be answered by wrestling with the question of a person's relation to God. For the questions posed by the abstraction "theism" are intensely personal and existential: Is there a God? Did he create me and does he care about me? How can I find God and know him?

Notes

[1] "The Pros and Cons of Theism: Whether They Constitute the Fundamental Issue of the Philosophy of Religion."

[2] Of course much philosophical discussion of theism gets removed pretty far from the concerns that give rise to the debates. As Westphal points out, discussions of middle-knowledge and divine simplicity have little bite for most ordinary people. However, even these abstruse discussions can be seen to have their origins in real-life concerns. Middle-knowledge, for example, is of interest to philosophers because some believe that it allows believers to consistently believe in both the sovereignty of God and the responsibility of human beings.

[3] Merold Westphal's *Suspicion and Faith: The Religious Uses of Modern Atheism* (Grand Rapids, Michigan: Wm. B. Eerdmans, 1993) is particularly recommended.

7
Theistic Argument and Edifying Discourse
Wayne Proudfoot

Alvin Plantinga nicely describes the philosophy of religion as just thinking hard about the central themes of religion.[1] But there are strong differences of opinion both about what themes are central and what constitutes hard thinking. I share the doubts of the other symposiasts about whether these differences can be captured in a dichotomy identified with the styles of the American Academy of Religion and the American Philosophical Association. But there are differences. For purposes of this paper, I will exaggerate those differences in order to contrast two types of approach to the subject.

Philosophers of religion whose primary affiliation is with the APA are more likely to identify themselves as analytic philosophers in the Anglo-American tradition, and those in the AAR as hermeneutic philosophers in the continental tradition, though that dichotomy has diminished in the past several decades. Members of each group often view the other as uncritical and naive, but the content of that criticism differs in the two cases. APA philosophers view those in the AAR as insufficiently rigorous in logic and argumentation, while those in the AAR view their counterparts as insufficiently historical.

Philosophers in the APA are more likely to be interested in the problems of traditional theism, and those in the AAR in religion as a social and cultural phenomenon, as well as in problems of comparative religion. This contrast is to some extent dependent upon fashions that change from decade to decade. The prominence since the early eighties of the Society of Christian Philosophers may lead us to identify all philosophy of religion in the APA with the work of its members, and with its focus on the problems of traditional theism and Christian doctrine. That would be a mistake, because there are philosophers in the APA who are thinking hard about other religious topics. Charles Taylor on *The Sources of the Self*, Jeffrie Murphy and Jean Hampton on *Forgiveness and Mercy*, and Moshe Halbertal and Avishai Margalit on *Idolatry* are some examples that come to mind. But sections on the philosophy of religion at annual meetings of the APA are more likely to revolve around the issues of traditional theism.

In the AAR, the topics and styles of thinking about religion represented in the section on philosophy of religion at the annual meeting are extremely diverse. "Philosophy of religion" in this context sometimes serves as a residual category for general reflection on religion, or on the history of religious ideas, that does not fit clearly into one of the sections identified by historical and regional location. Different sessions of the same section might be used to display different approaches to the field: phenomenological, process, analytic, feminist, comparative. Despite this diversity, however, little attention is paid to the problems of the coherence and rationality of traditional theism.

How is this difference to be accounted for? The most likely place to look is in the intellectual culture in which the philosopher is trained and with which she is professionally affiliated. Again, I want to exaggerate the differences in order to see whether we can account for some of the variance. The contrast I want to draw is meant to illumine a difference in intellectual context, in questions to be addressed, and in preferred literary genre.

Philosophers of religion in religion departments have usually been trained in graduate programs closely associated with theological faculties, or by faculty members who were themselves trained in a theological context. Advertisements for job openings in such departments usually call for someone in philosophy of religion, theology, or modern religious thought. These rubrics are regularly assimilated to one another. "Theology" is understood to be too parochial a term for a curriculum in the faculty of arts and sciences of a secular university, but otherwise no clear distinction is made between these terms.

The aim of a theological faculty is to train scholars and clergy to interpret a particular tradition in a way that makes it available for contemporary religious life. The approach is broadly hermeneutic. The study of the Bible is central and paradigmatic in a faculty of divinity. Scholarly tools are employed to understand the biblical text in its historic and linguistic context, and to serve historical reconstruction, informed exegesis, and theological reflection. Redescription of the tradition, informed by the best scholarship and contemporary needs and interests, is central to the task of a theological faculty. While the Bible is paradigmatic, study of church history, of the development of religious doctrine and practice, is also intended to achieve an understanding that will inform contemporary religious life.

For contemporary religious thought, this redescription of the tradition in the light of present interests and needs will focus most clearly on the relatively recent past. Protestant thought of the eighteenth and nineteenth centuries cannot be understood apart from the development of philosophy in that period. The canons that rule curricula and syllabi may pick out a philosophy track that revolves around epistemology and logic, with ancillary attention to ethics and political philosophy, and someone so inclined might also try to pick out a different track of "distinctively religious" thinkers during that period. But any course in the philosophy of religion would have to focus on some of the central figures of modern philosophy (e.g. Hume, Kant, Hegel), and would require acquaintance with the range of their thought. In this context, they would be read as critics of and contributors to modern religious thought.

These "philosophical" figures, along with others who are philosophically sophisticated but might be more readily situated in the "religious" track (e.g. Edwards, Schleiermacher, Kierkegaard), and still others who employ few philosophical tools are engaged in critical reflection upon religious thought and practice, from within and without, and redescriptions of religion and of religious doctrine. During most of the twentieth century, in American colleges and universities, these works were taught and this reflection continued largely in divinity schools, with some trickle down into the curricula of combined departments of religion and philosophy at liberal arts colleges. Those who teach philosophy of religion and modern religious thought in departments of religion are continuing this legacy.

Those who teach philosophy of religion in departments of philosophy have been trained in methods of contemporary philosophical analysis. They have studied epistemology, logic, ethics, and metaphysics, and often little, if any, philosophy of religion or religious thought. Advertisements for jobs in philosophy departments sometimes list philosophy of religion as an optional field of secondary competence, but rarely as the primary field of specialization. The Society of Christian Philosophers and *Faith and Philosophy* are evidence for and are to be credited with a revival of interest in the philosophy of religion. But the field is still often relegated to the periphery of the philosophical curriculum. Many of the figures who have been instrumental in the recent revival of interest in this field were trained and initially made their scholarly marks in other fields of philosophy. They then brought their philosophical methods and analytical expertise to bear on religious topics.

Much of the revived interest in philosophy of religion in departments of philosophy has centered around the issues of the rationality of religious belief, or the justification of that belief. This is, in part, a reflection of the centrality of epistemology in contemporary philosophy, and, in part, a reflection of the motivation of those who have focused their analytical skills on these topics. Nicholas Wolterstorff here, and others elsewhere, have said that when they entered the profession, they perceived that the only acceptable postures to take toward religious belief were neutrality or hostility.[2] Wolterstorff thinks that that attitude has changed recently, and attributes it to the demise of classically modern foundationalism. Now it is possible to show that religious belief is rationally acceptable. Some of the focus on traditional theism is motivated by a desire to show that those who subscribe to theistic beliefs are not violating any canons of logic or rational belief acquisition. These arguments serve as a defense; they parry criticism.

The appropriate literary genre for demonstrating the rational acceptability of religious belief is the philosophical argument. The language and style of the arguments employed in much of the recent literature on traditional theism is such as to suggest that they appeal only to universally accepted canons of rationality, and are independent of the religious stance of author or reader. Classical theism, identified in a particular way, is shown to be coherent. Belief in God is shown to rest on considerations analogous to, and no more vulnerable than, belief in other minds. Or the existence of God is shown to be, on the whole, more probable than not.

These analyses seem to assume that traditional theism, however identified, is a set of beliefs that is complete, and relatively self-contained. The description under which it is identified may be predicated on redescriptions of traditional doctrines, but it is usually not presented that way. For instance, Richard Swinburne writes that the claim that there is a God is to be understood in this way: "there exists necessarily and eternally a person essentially bodiless, omnipresent, creator and sustainer of any universe there may be, perfectly free, omnipotent, omniscient, perfectly good, and a source of moral obligation."[3] He adds that this view of God "has, with minor exceptions, been a central view of Western religion—Christianity, Judaism, and Islam."[4] In fact, highly anachronistic readings of the Bible and the Qur'an would be required in order to "discover" this view in those texts. The meanings of many of the constituent terms of that definition vary extensively across time and space, so as to render suspect the claim that this is a precise statement of the theism that has been common to those traditions. Swinburne is really inquiring about the coherence and acceptability of that set of beliefs he has constructed, and that is an appropriate inquiry. But his sweeping claim about the relation of that set to the history of monotheism in the west is unfounded.

If the most prominent genre in philosophical reflection on traditional theism is the argument for the coherence and rational acceptability of a particular set of beliefs, this contrasts greatly with much of the literature that is identified as philosophy of religion in the context of the AAR. Here the most prominent genre is not the philosophical argument, but the edifying discourse. This rhetorical style has its roots in contemporary religious thought. Much twentieth century Protestant theology is avowedly similar to preaching. Karl Barth regarded theology as witness to the word of God as revealed in Jesus Christ. Barth's *Letter to the Romans*, Reinhold Niebuhr's *Moral Man and Immoral Society*, H. Richard Niebuhr's *The Meaning of Revelation*, and Paul Tillich's *The Courage to Be* are all edifying discourses. This does not mean that they do not contain arguments, or are not philosophically sophisticated, but the genre is closer to the sermon or its secular counterpart, the broadly based university lecture, than to a paradigmatic logical argument.

In the middle decades of this century, while Anglo-American philosophers were increasingly employing techniques of logical or philosophical analysis and, like their colleagues in the sciences, were more likely to expect contributions to be published in tightly argued analytic articles than in books, Tillich, the Niebuhrs, and others were publishing with commercial presses for an audience that, in addition to their colleagues and students, consisted of a rather broad public, including colleagues in other fields, college students, and laity in the churches. Like the books mentioned above, these were edifying discourses. They often originated as lectures to a broadly based university audience, and were attempts to redescribe traditional religious doctrines and concepts in order to use them to illumine contemporary issues. These theologians all preached occasionally, and there is great overlap between the language and rhetoric of their sermons, their public lectures, and their theological treatises.

That period is past. But the generic influence lingers. The analytical article, with its precise definitions and rigorous argument, is no less stylized as a rhetorical device than the edifying discourse, but it is a different one. In the argument, one seeks precision and singular meaning. In the sermon or edifying discourse, multiple meanings are often employed and harmonics are set in motion to engage the listener. There is, of course, no reason to think that these styles are mutually exclusive. Philosophical arguments come in many different forms, some of which can be edifying. And a discourse cannnot be effective without some kind of argument. But the difference in genre does seem to capture something that still remains from the different genealogies of the two types of philosophy of religion.

Departments of religion are offspring of faculties of Protestant theology. Until recently, many mirrored in their curricula the divisions of theological education, with additional appointments for Asian religions. Philosophers of religion in these departments often carry on the legacy of philosophically informed historical and constructive theology. They intend their doctrines of God or conceptions of the religious life to be strong critical redescriptions of the tradition, and to shape that tradition in such a way as to make it available to serve the needs and interests of the present. That present is one that is increasingly shaped by knowledge of other religious traditions. These traditions are represented in the department of religion in a much more salient way than they were in the theological faculty, and redescriptions of religious experience, belief, and practice must take that new context into account. This is a different task from that of the analysis and criticism or defense of theism as a completed set of concepts and doctrines. Both are legitimate occasions for thinking hard about the central themes of religion.

Notes

[1] Alvin Plantinga, *God, Freedom, and Evil* (New York, 1974), p.1.

[2] See Nicholas Wolterstorff, "Between the Pincers of Increased Diversity and Supposed Irrationality," in this volume.

[3] Richard Swinburne, *The Christian God* (Oxford, 1994), pp. 125.

[4] Swinburne, *The Christian God*, p. 126.

8

Reflections on Analytical Philosophical Theology

Robert M. Adams

The present volume is a forum for commentary on a widespread impression that philosophers of religion whose primary professional home is in the American Philosophical Association (APA) are both likelier to be centrally concerned with issues about God, and likelier to be "traditional theists" themselves, than those who are primarily associated with the American Academy of Religion (AAR). I share this impression. One of the most frequent comments on it is that the interest in God is particularly associated with "analytical" philosophy of religion. I agree with that too, and my principal topic here will be the interest of analytical philosophers in theism.

First, however, I must acknowledge some misgivings I feel about the perceptions I share with other contributors to this volume. May they not be due in part to our ignoring some subcommunities within both the APA and the AAR? Not all members of the APA, by any means, are analytical philosophers; perhaps more attention to philosophy of religion done by some of those who are not would tend to soften the contrast with the AAR. And consider the case of process theology, which seems to me to be getting more of a hearing in the AAR than in the APA but is at least broadly theistic (I'd rather not debate whether it's "traditionally" theistic). I also wonder about the relation of our topic to the place of Christian theology, and analogous disciplines related to other religions, in the AAR and in the various sorts of academic departments to which AAR members belong; is the datum we're discussing an artifact, to any extent, of the way in which subfields are partitioned within the AAR? Perhaps not; some theologians seem to have the same sorts of reservations about analytical philosophy of religion that AAR philosophers tend to have.[1] On the other hand, a large proportion of those who work on ethics in the AAR seem quite at home with their (mainly analytical) counterparts in the APA. There are also questions about the ways in which responsibilities for philosophical theology are allocated to departments in Roman Catholic institutions, which have their own traditions distinguishing philosophy from theology. Neoscholasticism is a philosophical movement even friendlier to theism than analytical philosophy is; it also has an increasingly obvious affinity with analytical philosophy, which makes the boundary between neoscholastic and analytical philosophy of religion a fuzzy one. (It could also be said that analytical philosophy is itself a sort of scholasticism, in the logically disciplined, socially interactive manner of making progress on details that largely constitutes its wissenschaftlich character.)

It remains the case that many analytical philosophers (including me) are very interested in issues about God, and that in ways that seem old-fashioned to many members of the AAR. Why do we have this interest? Perhaps the first thing to be understood about us in this connection is that if analytical philosophy today is "post-" anything, it is postpositivist. 1995 is the fortieth anniversary year of the publication of *New Essays in Philosophical Theology*,[2] an internally diverse collection of papers that may plausibly be taken as marking the birth of analytical philosophy of religion, and of its preoccupation with theism. The central issue in that volume and in the first years of analytical philosophy of religion was religious language and its relation to the verifiability theory of meaning (the positivist thesis that no contingent statement has any "cognitive significance" except insofar as it is empirically testable). The verifiability theory was already on its way out, but was the classic formulation of a sort of empiricism to which most analytical philosophers were still committed.

1955 was the year in which I began the formal study of philosophy, and it is ironic now to remember that the feature of logical positivism, and hence of analytical philosophy, that seemed to me then to give most offense was what we would now call its antirealism—that is, the fact that the verifiability theory was meant to imply that neither truths nor genuine falsehoods are possible in metaphysics, ethics, and theology. Many of us who have subsequently become analytical philosophical theologians were already drawn to analytical philosophy by its clarity and rigor, and by the way in which it seemed to enable us to achieve wissenschaftlich progress, and even a surprising measure of agreement—if not about the big issues, then at least about what the problems are and what are the strengths and weaknesses of the various arguments. Despite the formidable obstacle posed by the arguments and concerns surrounding the verifiability theory, we hoped that the methods of analytical philosophy might be used to achieve some progress with regard to theological questions—and I believe these hopes have been realized in significant measure over the last forty years.

The irony that I find today in these memories is a role-reversal. Much of the criticism of analytical philosophy that I hear now comes from the strong antimetaphysical stream in Continental European philosophy, and is directed precisely against the realism regarding metaphysical issues now embraced by many analytical philosophers—a realism that seems naively "pre-Kantian" to many of our critics. I will not try to chronicle the changes on the "nonanalytical"[3] side that contributed to this role reversal. I suppose the growing influence of Marx, Nietzsche, and Freud and the waning influence of the likes of Bradley and Whitehead has something to do with it. Perhaps also in my youthful inexperience I misperceived the situation in the fifties; perhaps the antirealism was not even then the main sticking point in logical positivism for its critics in general. It certainly was the main sticking point for me; but perhaps there were many who had no love for metaphysics but thought that the wissenschaftlich character of analytical philosophy, which appealed so much to me, was not nearly geisteswissenschaftlich enough. But I will not worry about that side of the history here.

I am more concerned to make the point that the metaphysical realism of many analytical philosophers is not so much pre-Kantian as post-positivist. The most formative experience of analytical philosophy as it exists today may well have been the logical empiricists' critique of their own theories about meaning. Important papers of the early fifties—notably Hempel's critique of existing formulations of the verifiability criterion and Quine's critique of the analytic/synthetic distinction[4]—led in time to the abandonment of the verifiability theory. Hempel and many others were still broadly committed to the antimetaphysical empiricism to which the theory had given form. But it had become clear that the antimetaphysical stance was not unproblematic, and this gave courage for more and more openly metaphysical essays. Eventually "metaphysics" ceased to be used as a term of opprobrium and has become the name of a respected field in analytical philosophy, a field in which jobs are advertised and tenure is granted. This is not to deny that many analytical philosophers hold antimetaphysical or antirealist views; many do. But I think it is now widely agreed in analytical philosophy that antimetaphysical views require defense just as much as metaphysical views do, and that no view in these matters is easy to defend. In the wake of the demise of the verifiability theory, the older critiques of metaphysics by Hume and Kant no longer seem beyond question either (which is not to say that they are easily dismissed).

We analytical philosophers are not all empiricists any more. We do not all identify philosophy with linguistic analysis (so the label "analytical" may be misleading, though it will probably not be abandoned soon). Indeed I think we do not now share any substantive philosophical doctrine, but only a discipline or style of doing philosophy. Most of the main positions in the history of Western philosophy can be and are articulated and defended in an analytical context. There are materialists, dualists, and idealists among us. There are nominalists and platonists. There are also theists and atheists.

Theism is a metaphysical thesis, and attention to questions about God has been an important part of the revival of metaphysics within analytical philosophy. The historic arguments for God's existence, for example, have been reexamined with a rigor that I believe enables us to understand them better than they have been understood before.[5] I have the impression that it is widely assumed in religious studies, and even in theology, that these arguments can simply be dismissed, on the basis of the critique to which they were subjected by Hume and Kant. Undoubtedly a majority of analytical philosophers, including some who are theists, would accept a negative verdict on the arguments; but there is a substantial body of opinion that refuses simply to dismiss them. Hardly anyone thinks that any one argument, all by itself, conclusively "proves" the existence of God, but many think that some of them can play an important part in a "cumulative case" for theism. The question of their probative force has been reopened and remains a live issue for discussion. I think one of the lessons of analytical philosophical experience thus far is that conclusive demonstration is not to be expected on major philosophical issues—which does not mean that we cannot make progress in understanding them, and in coming to reasoned conclusions for ourselves.

A major event in the history of recent analytical metaphysics which has had a constructive impact on philosophical theology is the explosive development of modal logic and the philosophy of possibility and necessity in the 1970s. This development probably did as much as anything else to give analytical philosophers courage for heady metaphysical speculation. It has contributed quite specifically to a new examination of issues about the divine attributes, enabling us to take seriously, and understand with some precision, ideas about essential predication of which earlier analytical philosophy had been unable to make sense. In giving currency to ideas of a metaphysical and not merely linguistic or conventional necessity, moreover, the philosophical discussion of modal logic has helped to revive interest in the idea of necessary divine existence.[6] The increasingly sophisticated interest of analytical philosophers in the history of philosophy has also fed into the interest in theism. We have always had a canon of "great dead philosophers," from Plato to Kant, whom we have used in our teaching and from whom we have derived, in no small measure, the problems on which we work. The study of these authors has increasingly become a specialty as rigorous historically and exegetically as it is philosophically, and it has become increasingly difficult to ignore the central role that questions, ideas, and arguments about God play in most of the philosophical classics. For those of us who are ready enough to disagree with Descartes and Leibniz, but not to take a dismissive attitude toward them, it is harder to take a dismissive attitude toward the ontological argument, for example.

In these considerations we find one of the sources of analytical philosophers' interest in theism: it is a central topic, and one of the most fascinating topics, in the Western (and not only the Western) metaphysical tradition. It is an object of absorbing interest to people who love metaphysics, whether or not they are religious. It is also an object that many of us can hardly fail to encounter in the course of teaching philosophy to undergraduates. One of the major reasons for studying theism is similar to the classic reason for climbing Mt. Everest: because it's there. The topic of the nature of necessity, mentioned above, is one of very limited human interest except insofar as one is interested in metaphysics and the philosophy of logic, but it has often held the most intense interest of metaphysicians. Similarly issues about God can be expected to interest metaphysicians whether or not these issues are "where the action is" in religious thought. There may not be any living philosopher who has been convinced of the truth of theism by studying the ontological argument, for example, but many philosophers are still fascinated with the argument. It is one of the most ingenious in the history of philosophy, and a thing of beauty in the eyes of some of us, whether or not it proves the existence of God.

This is not to deny, of course, that religious motives play a part in the interest in theism among analytical philosophers (as anywhere else that it is found). For some, faith in God is the center of life; for others, perhaps, a fascinating personal possibility. What better reasons could there be for an interest in theism? If philosophers have such personal relations to theism, why would they not want to have a philosophical understanding of it?

With these obvious reasons for interest in theism, and with the opportunities that analytical philosophy affords for pursuing that interest, why hasn't analytical philosophical theology attracted more attention in religious studies? I might be tempted to think it is simply the intrinsic difficulty of much analytical philosophy, or too slight an initiation into analytical philosophy to appreciate its opportunities. But I fear there is more to it than that. I am convinced that the topics in which analytical philosophy of religion has been interested are crucially important for the viability of several religious traditions, but there are also important ways in which these analytical interests really are narrow from the point of view of religious studies, and even from the perspective of Christian theology.

The most obvious of these, the Eurocentrism of analytical philosophy, has no deep grounds that I can see in the nature of our discipline, though the human difficulty of overcoming it is not to be underestimated. I have no doubt that the disciplines of analytical philosophy can be as fruitfully applied to Indian philosophical and religious texts and ideas, for example, as they have been to Western ones; and we ought to be doing more of that. For an American to do it, however, typically involves two arduous apprenticeships: in analytical philosophy and in the languages and texts of a non-Western tradition.

Another limitation may be more deeply rooted in analytical philosophy. Theism is at most one aspect of any living religious tradition. By itself it is much too thin a soup to constitute a religion, as religious thinkers from Schleiermacher to the present day have emphasized. Many analytical philosophers of religion are well aware of this point, and a number of them have recently devoted considerable effort to philosophical examination of such Christian doctrines as those of the Trinity, christology, and the atonement, which go far beyond "mere" theism into "revealed" theology. These efforts have generally assumed quite traditional conceptions of the doctrines, and have concentrated on problems of formulation and defense that are broadly related to issues in metaphysics and moral philosophy. I am convinced that this is worth doing. If these topics are comparatively neglected by theologians today, that is all the more reason for philosophers to take up the task when they have something to contribute. So long as they take this form, however, our studies of Christian doctrines may fail to make contact with one of the central preoccupations of many theologians and students of religion: the reinterpretation of religious traditions.

Reinterpretation of tradition, arguably, is and always has been a feature of any living theology, or indeed of any living appropriation of religious tradition. In Western religious thought of the last two centuries this process has become exceptionally self-conscious. Reinterpretation of religious traditions has taken place in a context of historical and theoretical study of tradition as such, of its symbolic and institutional embodiments, of culture (more broadly), and of processes of change in all these matters. In this context the study of religion has tended to focus on such questions as the following: What is a religious tradition? What is the essence of a given religious tradition? What are its boundaries (if it has any)? What is the role of belief, in religious traditions? What constitutes holding the same belief, in different historical and cultural contexts? What is the meaning of traditional texts, ceremonies, and doctrines today? And in the light of such questions, what constitutes loyalty to a tradition? It is clear that the branches of philosophy bearing most directly on such questions are hermeneutics, philosophical sociology, and the philosophy of history. Analytical philosophers have contributed much less than others to these fields, and thus may seem to religionists to have relatively little to say about some of the philosophical issues that most interest them. This may change; analytical techniques might well be fruitfully applied to many of these issues, and the 21st century may see a development of analytical philosophy in these domains. As of now, however, it is natural for students of religion to look to other philosophical sources for light on these matters.

It is possible that there is a more permanent tension between analytical discipline and the interest in reinterpretation of tradition, inasmuch as they give rise to contrasting attitudes toward ambiguity. Striving for clarity, analytical study of a traditional doctrine tends to focus on at most a few very clear-cut lines of interpretation, whereas commitment to continual reinterpretation may make one more interested in retaining the open-ended possibilities inherent in a penumbra of meaning. What from one point of view makes a doctrine clear enough to be intelligently discussed may seem from another mainly to make it more one-dimensional. The legitimate interest in clarifying a topic may clash with a legitimate reluctance to give up a kaleidoscopic richness of meanings. Because familiar thoughts are likely to be clearer than those that are just being born, it is probably true that the more "clear-cut" positions are likely also to be more "conservative," and the analytically inclined need to be conscious of that bias. I refuse to believe that the interests of clarity and reinterpretation are irreconcilable; but reconciling them will require patient attention to both families of concerns—an effort that can never be finished, by virtue of the dynamics of reinterpretation.

Of the various approaches or schools of thought within analytical philosophy of religion, the one that has found the most favor among theologians and students of religion is the Wittgensteinian. I suspect that is largely due to a perceived compatibility of Wittgensteinianism with the interest in traditions and their reinterpretation. The Wittgensteinian emphasis on the social basis of meanings is congenial to these theological interests; so is the soft antirealism of many Wittgensteinian treatments of religious doctrines. For antirealism has much the same advantage for reinterpretation that ambiguity has. A realist construal of a religious doctrine is relatively univocal as to the main function of the doctrinal affirmation: it is meant to state a fact. An antirealist construal denies that, and opens a question as to what is the main function of the doctrinal formula. The hostile answer, that the doctrine is sheer nonsense and has no useful function, is possible; but so are friendlier answers. Perhaps an emotive expressive analysis will be given, or a social structural analysis; the floor is open for suggestions.

One attraction of such antirealist approaches is that a conservative retention of traditional credal and liturgical formulas can be combined with a more or less radical reinterpretation of their function. As a religious person I am reluctant to accept this bargain. More of the substance of my religious tradition, in my opinion, is likely to be given up in such a wholesale abandonment of truth claims than in a piecemeal modification of traditional formulas and their detailed interpretation.

This judgment must be modified, however, by the observation that the issue between realism and antirealism is not all-or-nothing. Realism and antirealism can be topic-relative, and usually are; one can be a realist on one subject and an antirealist on others. Some analytical philosophers are realists about physical objects and antirealists about ethics, for instance; and the opposite view has considerable appeal for me. It is likewise possible to be a realist about some theological issues and an antirealist (or much less of a realist) about others. Indeed, the vocabulary of "realism" and "antirealism" is probably too crude to deal with the full array of ways in which we might think of affirmations as related to truth and falsity.

Both the "APA" projects and the "AAR" projects that I have discussed here seem to me well worth pursuing, and we all have much to learn by attending to each others' methods and interests. Still, such attention is not likely to convert many of us from theism to nontheism or vice versa, from realism to antirealism or vice versa. And we cannot expect theists and nontheists, realists and antirealists, to find the same topics equally interesting.

Notes

1 See, e.g., Gordon D. Kaufman, "'Evidentialism': A Theologian's Response," *Faith and Philosophy* 6 (1989): 35–46.

2 Edited by Antony Flew and Alasdair MacIntyre (London: SCM Press, 1955).

3 "Nonanalytical philosophy" is doubtless an even unhappier term than "analytical philosophy," but I don't see a convenient alternative to it here.

4 Hempel's seminal contributions are reprinted in Carl G. Hempel, *Aspects of Scientific Explanation and Other Essays in the Philosophy of Science* (New York: Free Press, 1965), pp. 101–19. See also Willard Van Orman Quine, "Two Dogmas of Empiricism," *The Philosophical Review* 60 (1951): 20–43.

5 For examples, all analytical in mode, see William L. Rowe, *The Cosmological Argument* (Princeton: Princeton University Press, 1975) (nonpartisan); Richard Swinburne, *The Existence of God* (Oxford: Clarendon Press, 1979: revised edition 1991) (theistic); J. L. Mackie, *The Miracle of Theism: Arguments For and Against the Existence of God* (Oxford: Clarendon Press, 1982) (atheistic); and Robert Merrihew Adams, *The Virtue of Faith and Other Essays in Philosophical Theology* (New York: Oxford University Press, 1987), chs. 10, 15, 16 (theistic).

6 Cf. Alvin Plantinga, *The Nature of Necessity* (Oxford: Clarendon Press, 1974), esp. chs. 9–10, and Adams, *The Virtue of Faith*, chs. 13–14.